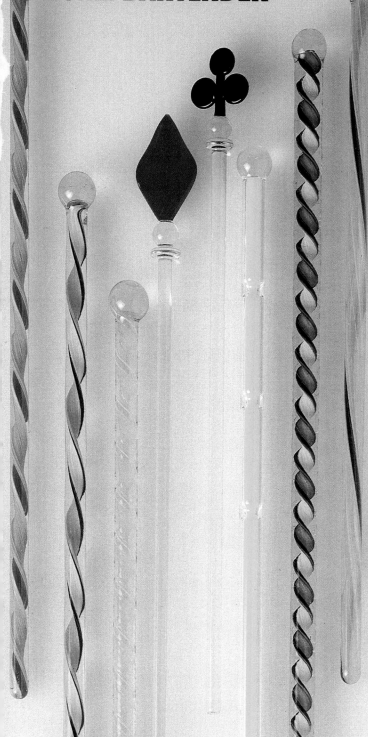

HOME BARTENDER

HOME BARTENDER

Rosalind Cooper

Hamlyn
London · New York · Sydney · Toronto

Published 1984 by The Hamlyn Publishing
Group Limited
London · New York · Sydney · Toronto
Astronaut House, Feltham, Middlesex,
England

By arrangement with Nicholas Enterprises Ltd

© Copyright Nicholas Enterprises Limited 1984

ISBN 0 600 32446 X

Printed in Italy by
Arti Grafiche VINCENZO BONA - Torino

CONTENTS

‖NTRODUCTION‖

In this book you will find all you need to know about setting up a bar at home, including choosing equipment, glasses and bottles. More important, the book includes a comprehensive range of recipes for mixed drinks of all kinds, as well as indications of how to serve even the most unusual spirits, wines and beers.

The book is divided into sections according to the spirit under discussion. First of all, you will find the most commonly used spirits – WHISKEY, VODKA, GIN, RUM and BRANDY. Each section contains full details on the various types available with plenty of recipes for using the spirit at home. There is also a guide to the major brands, both American and European, with reference to Australia and Africa. TEQUILA also has a separate section because it is fast becoming a popular drink worldwide. Here it is compared with other fruit and vegetable spirits of the world.

After these sections, there is a section on LIQUEURS, including some of the very newest such as Baileys Irish Cream, and some of the oldest, dating back to medieval days. Each is clearly described and there are many ideas for their use in the kitchen and the drinks cabinet. BITTERS are also treated, as Campari and other brands are of great importance for the home bartender, and Angostura bitters is a vital element of so many mixed drinks. You will also find the anise drinks such as Pernod here.

WINES are growing in popularity, with many drinkers now choosing them in preference to spirits. The section on TABLE WINES will give you a good idea of which wines should accompany certain foods, and how to serve red, white and rosé wines. SPARKLING WINES, including champagne, are not just for celebrations. You may be surprised to see how many lovely mixed drinks may be made with these charming wines. FORTIFIED WINES include such standbys as vermouth, sherry and Maderia. All three are useful in the kitchen and the bar.

BEER and CIDER are not neglected in this book nor are those who choose not to drink alcohol. In the MIXERS section there are plenty of ideas for delicious "Alternative Cocktails" made with fruit juice and fizzy mixers.

Finally, there's a section devoted to PARTIES. This gives hints on how to use the drinks you have read about in your own entertaining. Each party idea also suggests appropriate snacks as accompaniments, and there is a brief guide to good party-giving for the attentive host.

Gibson Martini

HOW TO USE THIS BOOK

The book is arranged so that recipes relate directly to the spirit under discussion. For instance, you will find a **Manhattan** in the WHISKEY section, and **Piña Colada** in the section on RUM. When you are not sure where your favourite drink fits into the scheme, simply consult the comprehensive Index at the end of this book.

Various symbols have been used with the recipes, as an instant visual guide to the drinks and how to serve them. They are:

GLASSES

Y cocktail glass

♀ wine globlets

▢ short tumbler

▯ tall tumbler (highball glass)

☕ punch cup *or* beer tankard

♀ brandy balloon glass

▯ champagne glass

PREPARATION

 cocktail shaker required

blender required

drink is stirred with a spoon

ALCOHOLIC STRENGTH

A star system is used so that you can choose the right drink to fit the occasion and make sure no one has too much to drink! Roughly speaking, each star is equivalent to one shot of spirit. Of course, drinks with a lower alcohol content use fewer expensive ingredients and are therefore a better value.

☆ equivalent to one shot of spirit or one glass of wine.

☆ ☆ equivalent to two shots of spirit.

☆ ☆ ☆ equivalent to three shots of spirit.

STANDARD MEASURES

Throughout the book, a measure is the same as a jigger, i.e. 1.5 fluid ounces (4 cl).

 A ''dash'' is not standardized but could be described as one-eighth of a teaspoon.

DRINKS & DRINKING

Serving drinks at home is a tradition as old as hospitality itself. An attractively served drink with just the right balance of alcohol makes your guest, invited or impromptu, feel at ease and welcome. Today's cocktail party is a direct descendant of gatherings of ancient Greeks, Egyptians or Romans.

These cultures knew about wine-making and also how to distill the wine into spirit. But really drinkable spirit was not made until some centuries later, when people realized that double distillation made the drink smoother. Before this time, rough spirit was often used as a medicine rather than a social drink. Alternatively, it was mixed with sweeteners and flavourings to make an early form of liqueur. Monks, with their knowledge of herbs, became the experts at this process and even today they are the makers of some of the world's finest liqueurs.

St. Patrick is said to have taught the Irish how to make *potheen*, a simple form of whiskey, and the Scots learned from their cousins. This knowledge soon travelled to the New World with the early settlers and both Canada and the United States soon had their own styles of whiskey, made with rye or corn, rather than the European barley.

The so-called "white spirits," including gin and vodka, also have many centuries of history behind them. Vodka was the drink of Tsars for hundreds of years before its rise to popularity in the Western world over the last 60 years. Gin was the drink of the London poor before reform improved its quality and created the drink we know today as London Dry Gin.

Rum has long been associated with sailors, and even pirates, in the Caribbean area. Their favourite drink was dark brown and gave the sensation of warming, a far cry from the sophisticated and smooth white rum which is a bestseller now.

Brandy is also associated with travel, and many people believe it helps cure a queasy stomach on a journey. Brandy was first made when it was discovered that distilling wine made it easier to ship and keep in good condition – hence its name, which means "burnt wine."

In general, as the years have passed, popular taste has tended toward lighter styles of drink. In the 1980s this trend has reached a point where many drinkers prefer the lighter spirits such as vodka and white rum in mixed drinks, and some have given up spirits altogether, favouring dry white wine, which is low in calories but perhaps a little less exciting in flavour.

Cocktails have potential for some truly fascinating flavour combinations. Many of the classic blends were created during the years of Prohibition in America when illegal "hooch" was very crude and needed added flavours to disguise its roughness. But once the Volstead Act was repealed, cocktails were here to stay, and could only improve with practice. And, ever improving brands of spirits became available.

In the world of drinks, some brands have almost mystical significance; for example, *Beefeater's* for gin or *Cutty Sark* for Scotch.

This too dates from the days of the Speakeasy when these British spirits were not officially allowed to be sold, but when obtained were certainly better than the U.S. version. Today, of course, it is a different story. Some of the world's top selling brands of spirits are American or Canadian, with a reputation for very high quality.

While buying the well-known brand means you are getting a reliable product, it sometimes pays to look at the alternatives – using a "house-bottled" spirit, vermouth or mixer can save you a great deal of money, and mixed in cocktails they are usually just as agreeable to drink.

MEASURES OF ALCOHOLIC STRENGTH

%GL	US Proof	UK Proof
10	20	11.5
20	40	35

Table wines are under 20 GL.

30	60	52.50

Some liqueurs are 30 GL, also pastis and some aperitif drinks.

40	80	70

This is the usual strength for most spirits, e.g. whiskey, gin, rum and vodka.

41	82	71.75
42	84	73.50
43	86	75.25

41-43 are so-called "export-strength spirits."

50	100	87.50

Remember that 100 on a U.S. bottle does not mean 100% alcohol, only 50% by volume.

57.14	114.28	100
60	120	105

1.50 litre

1 litre

PROOF

Proof is a way of describing the exact alcohol content in any spirit or wine. The easiest system to understand is that created by a Frenchman named Gay-Lussac, which measures the amount of pure alcohol in a given volume of spirit or wine. The percentage of alcohol is then expressed on a scale from 0% (which would be pure water) to 100% (pure alcohol). A typical bottle of spirit would be around 40 G.L. (Gay-Lussac), equivalent to 80 US proof (see table opposite).

Americans and British use the term proof differently. In the United States the proof value is simply twice the alcohol strength, thus 100 US proof is 50 G.L. (50 per cent alcohol by volume). The British system is old-fashioned and more complex. See the accompanying table for a comparison and be sure to check the label of any bottle you buy for the country of origin.

THE IMPORTANCE OF AGING

Both wines and spirits may benefit from aging in wood casks. To a lesser extent they also age in glass bottles, but this does not apply to those spirits and wines (e.g. vermouth) which are sold in bottles sealed at the time of shipment. Alcoholic drinks age as a result of air mingling with them. As air passes through the staves of a cask, or the pores of cork, a chemical reaction gradually takes place to alter the flavour and appearance of the drink, giving a "mellower" taste. This is especially desirable for whiskies, brandies and red wines. White wines need little if any aging as their freshness is appealing; white spirits such as rum and vodka are aged for relatively short periods simply to smooth out any "raw" qualities in the spirit.

.75 litre

375 millilitres

BOTTLE SIZES

The standard bottle size worldwide is now .75 litre (25.4 fluid ounces). This goes for both wines and spirits. You will probably also find a litre size in many popular brands, and sometimes a litre and a half (equivalent to two standard bottles). In the United States the 1.75 litre bottle is common, equivalent to 59.2 fluid ounces. Smaller bottles may be a useful purchase for a rarely-used liqueur or costly spirit. The half-bottle (375 millilitres or 12.7 fluid ounces) is a handy and manageable size. See the following pages for advice on what sizes to purchase, and what measures to serve.

THE HOME BAR

Setting up a bar at home is not difficult. All you need is a few bottles of basic spirits and some mixers, with glasses and ice, and you have a "bar." But of course you can make your bar much more sophisticated than that. There are now shops which sell nothing but gadgets for making cocktails at home and you could spend a great deal of money on these. So what is necessary and what is a luxury?

THE CHOICE OF BOTTLES

Your selection may be limited at first by what you can afford. The secret of a good bartender is ingenuity, so make the most of the ingredients you have on hand. First of all, you will need the essential spirit, the heart of a good cocktail. Every cocktail consists of a base (the spirit), a modifier, and a colouring or flavouring agent. Soda is a finishing touch. For example, a **Manhattan** is based on whiskey, with vermouth added as a modifier, and finally some Angostura bitters as an added colouring and flavouring agent.

Other examples of modifiers are fruit juices, wine, sugar, cream and eggs. They smooth out the texture of the drink and take away the fiery quality of the spirit. Colouring and flavoring agents include various fruit syrups (for example, grenadine), liqueurs and bitters.

Start your bar with the most versatile spirits: gin, whiskey, white rum and vodka. With these four you can produce an extraordinary number of mixed drinks with just a few additional ingredients. To start with, these should include:

Soda or mineral water
Cointreau or Triple Sec orange liqueur
Apricot brandy
Crème de cacao (white or dark)
Galliano liqueur
Grenadine syrup
Fruit juices (orange, pineapple, lemon)
Angostura bitters
Worcestershire sauce
Tabasco
Vermouth (sweet and dry)

With these few ingredients, you will be able to produce a good range of cocktails including:

The **Dry Martini**, the **Manhattan**, the **Harvey Wallbanger**, the **Screwdriver, Mai Tai, Piña Colada** and many others.

If your budget is sufficient you might consider adding a bottle of three-star French brandy, ideal for a **Brandy Alexander**, and perhaps tequila for making a **Margarita** or **Tequila Sunrise**. One way to afford these is to limit your purchase of liqueurs to half-bottles. These will be used only gradually and in tiny quantities.

For the guest who prefers wine, it is a good idea to begin a collection of reliable bottles of inexpensive red and white table wine, perhaps a good *Vin de Pays* from France, a *Soave* or *Valpolicella* from Italy, or a *Chablis* and *Burgundy* from a top-ranked California winery. Add to these a couple of bottles of sparkling wine, and your shopping list is complete. Other and more exotic bottles may be added as opportunity arises or for a theme party.

Your kitchen cupboard and refrigerator are also sources for important ingredients for some drinks. You may need cream, which should be the heavy kind and always very fresh, or eggs for certain drinks. Salt and pepper is used for spicy drinks such as the **Bloody Mary**. Fresh fruit is important as a garnish, particularly lemons, oranges and pineapple. Cocktail cherries are attractive in many classic cocktails, and of course sugar or sugar syrup (see page 21) is added to many mixtures.

EQUIPMENT FOR THE HOME BAR

Start at the beginning and consider how you make a drink. First you will need to open the bottles. A **corkscrew** will be useful, as will be a bottle opener for beers and mixers. The so-called ''waiter's friend'' combines both functions and for that reason is very popular with professional bartenders.

Next, you mix the drink. According to the style of cocktail, you may need no special equipment at all, but a shaker, blender or mixing jug may be useful. **Cocktail shakers** are very attractive and may be displayed as one of the features of a home bar. Those made of polished metal are very stylish and also eminently practical. You simply remove the cap and put ice cubes into the base.

This is then filled with the various ingredients which are shaken together to produce a well-balanced cocktail. In general, the shaker makes a slightly cloudier drink than one which is stirred – hence all the debate about how to make Martinis!

Many cocktail shakers also incorporate a **strainer**. The drink is filtered through this as it is poured into the glass. You may want to use a proper bartender's strainer, called a Hawthorne strainer. This gadget is made of metal with an edge of rolled wire to prevent spilling as you gently strain the cocktail after shaking or stirring.

If stirring is called for, then use a **glass cup** or **large tumbler** to prepare the drink. Use a **long-handled spoon** and always remember to stir very gently. In this way you will preserve the delicate flavour of the various ingredients of your cocktail.

Rich and creamy cocktails, especially some of those made with rum are made with a **blender**. One important feature to note is that these cocktails need a base of crushed ice to give them their thick texture. So you will need a blender that can cope with ice cubes. To aid crushing of the ice, crack it first with an ice pick or crush it gently in a tea towel with a wooden mallet. This last method is also useful if you need crushed ice to add to a finished drink.

When you give a cocktail party, make sure ice is plentiful. Keep some in an **ice bucket** for your guests to use as required. An ice bucket is also useful when serving champagne, sparkling wine or white wines . When you offer ice to your guests, it is a nice touch to use ice tongs or your guests may get cold and wet before long!

The fruit juices used in many of the drinks mentioned in these pages may be obtained from your local market in bottles or cartons, but freshly-squeezed juices have superior flavour. A good investment is a juicing attachment for a mixer, or a free-standing **citrus juicer**, which speeds the work of the traditional lemon squeezer.

Lemons are also used as a garnish, so an obvious item of equipment you will need is a **small sharp knife**. A special chopping board should be reserved for this purpose.

GLASSES & MEASURES

All the recipes for mixed drinks in this book use a system of measures rather than giving precise fluid ounces or centilitres. It is far easier to use a standard measure than it is to pour the ingredients into a measuring cup each time. The standard measure is usually known as a "jigger," which holds 4 centilitres or 1½ fluid ounces. Jiggers may be bought at any specialist cocktail accessory shops, or you can use any small glass you have at home, providing you always use the same glass.

Whether you rent or buy the glasses for your party, it is worth considering which drink you plan to serve in them. Most cocktails have a traditional shape of glass which sets off the appearance of the drink and suits their style. For example, a drink with ice needs a taller glass.

Left to right: standard measure (jigger) 1½fl oz (4cl), highball glass 10fl oz (28cl), rocks glass 5fl oz (14cl), cocktail glass 4½fl oz (13cl), goblet 4fl oz (11cl), tulip wine glass 8fl oz (23cl), Paris goblet 8fl oz (23cl).

But it is sometimes more difficult to decide which glass to use.

In general, any spirit served straight without ice is served in a small, stemmed glass, like the traditional liqueur glass. This is especially suitable for vodka, aquavit and, of course, liqueurs. Whiskies are always served in tumblers, and look particularly well in cut glass or crystal. Even a fine whisky without ice is usually served in this type of glass in Britain. The adding of ice or soda makes the short tumbler look just right. Many whiskey-based cocktails also use this tumbler, although some do specify the Martini-style cocktail glass.

A **cocktail glass** has a long stem and a clear bowl so that the drink may be admired for its colour and viscosity. The stem keeps the drink away from the warmth of the drinker's hand and the drink stays cool for as long as possible. By contrast, a tumbler is held in the hand but ice can be added so the drink will hold its chill longer. A typical cocktail glass holds about 13 cl. (4½ fluid ounces), and a short tumbler about 14 cl. (5 fluid ounces). The tumbler may also be described as an Old Fashioned glass or a **rocks glass**.

Tall drinks made with spirits, or simply with fruit juices and mixers are served in a tall tumbler, also known as a **highball glass** or a Collins glass. A 28 cl.

Left to right: fluted champagne glass 5fl oz (14cl), sherry glass 5fl oz (14cl), brandy glass 10fl oz (28cl), liqueur glass 1fl oz (3cl), Punch cup 7fl oz (20cl), beer tankard 13fl oz (36cl).

(10 fl. oz.) size is appropriate for most of these drinks. This is a versatile glass in the home, used for beer and even iced tea or soda as well as cocktails.

Wines call for their own style of glass. Like the cocktail glass, this should have a stem so that the wine is held clear of the hand and may be seen clearly. Never use a tinted wine glass. A simple goblet, often called a **Paris goblet**, which holds about 23 cl. (8 fl. oz.) is the most useful for general purposes. It is also handy for certain cocktails, such as those made with cream.

Champagne and brandy have their own glasses. Use a **balloon shape for brandy** to enhance appreciation of its fine aroma, but keep to a small size. If you use the giant goblets offered in restaurants, you will lose all the scent and have to pour enormous servings. For sparkling wines, a tall glass, known as the **"flute"** in France, is ideal. The old-fashioned flat "coupe" is rarely used now but can be attractive for creamy cocktails.

CARE OF GLASSES

All your bartender's equipment should be maintained with care, but glasses need particular attention. Wash them in very hot water with just a little detergent, too much can stain the glass, or use the delicate cycle of your dishwasher. Allow glasses to dry fully before putting them away. The ideal method for drying is to hang glasses upside down and let the air dry them naturally, but using a dishwasher overcomes this problem. If you need to wash glasses during a party, make sure your drying cloth is lint-free and preferably made of linen.

GARNISHES

The various fruit and vegetable garnishes for each mixed drink are described with the recipe. These include lemons, oranges, pineapple, celery, cocktail cherries and olives. Mint is another useful garnish, but this should be fresh from the garden. If you have no garden, consider growing some on a balcony or in a window box.

The amusing final touches to a drink can include paper umbrellas, stirrers and straws. Use these for parties to add colour and style, but be careful not to overload a drink.

PRACTICAL TIPS

There are ways of making drinks served at home look just as good as those served in a bar. Most of them are simple "tricks" used by professional bartenders with great effect.

How to chill and frost a glass

For instance, before your guests arrive, put all the glasses you plan to use for cocktails into the freezer and allow to chill (this is also very effective for beer glasses). They will then have a frosted appearance and keep the drink cooler longer. Similarly, put your "white spirits" such as vodka, gin and white rum into the freezer for a few hours. This will change their appearance so that they become slightly "oily." Many Martini drinkers swear this improves their favourite drink.

Use ice cleverly. Crushed ice gives a drink style, as does a drink made with ice in the blender (try a **Daquiri** mixed in the blender with fresh fruit). Freeze ice into interesting shapes, not just the plain cube. You can also freeze fruit juices to add flavour and colour.

Certain drinks, such as a **Margarita**, call for a glass frosted with salt. Cut a slice of lemon or lime and rub it around the rim of a cocktail glass. Pour fine ground salt into a mound, then gently press the damp rim of the glass into the salt until you have an even coat. This method may also be used to coat the rim of a glass with sugar for rich cocktails, or for simple mixes such as gin and orange juice. Use super-fine ground sugar or castor sugar, or grind granulated sugar in your blender for cocktail uses.

Adding sugar

Adding sugar to drinks can be difficult – it dissolves slowly at times. Bartenders use sugar syrup (known as *gommé* to professionals). To make your own at home, put equal parts of sugar and water into a pan, and heat slowly. Bring the mixture to a boil and simmer for a minute. Allow it to cool, then pour into a bottle. Store in a cool place.

How to twist a lemon

A very sophisticated garnish, especially in a **Martini**, is the twist of lemon or orange peel. Use a very sharp knife to cut a thin strip of peel from the fruit. Twist it between your thumb and forefinger as you hold it

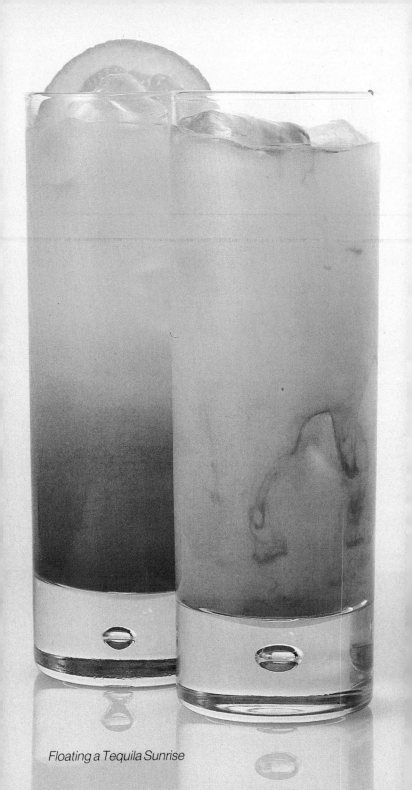

Floating a Tequila Sunrise

over the drink to release a little oil from the peel. Then drop the twist into the finished cocktail.

How to flame spirits

Spirits may be flamed for a variety of reasons. At the dinner table, you may wish to add drama to a special dessert or main dish by flaming with brandy or a liqueur. Crepes Suzette, for example, are always made with an orange liqueur. Or you may want to add subtle richness in the kitchen by flaming a dish such as Coq au Vin or Beef Daube with brandy during the cooking. The alcohol is ''burnt off'' during flaming, leaving the aroma of the spirit and added richness.

The secret of flaming is to ensure the spirit is warm. If you simply wish to flame a liqueur you will drink (e.g. Sambuca, with its added coffee bean) then warm the glass of liqueur over a spirit lamp or gas jet for a few seconds, then light carefully. Use a taper held at arm's length rather than a match for safety reasons. Similarly warm the spirit for flaming meat dishes, but beware of the flames from hot fat.

For Crepes Suzette and other sweets like Cherries Jubilee, add sugar and spirit at the same time and this will give a longer-lasting flame, also adding caramel to the finished dessert. Delicious and spectacular for your guests, yet this idea uses only a tiny amount of the liqueur you will have ready in your home bar.

How to float cordials or liqueurs

Attractive effects may be achieved by floating one spirit on top of another. The two merge together to give a streaky look, then separate out into layers. Always pour in the heaviest drink first, i.e. the one with most sugar. If the drink calls for a syrup such as grenadine, then this would be first; alternatively pour the liqueur first. Use chilled bottles to increase the density of the drinks (freezing heightens the effect, especially for drinks with white spirits such as vodka and gin). One of the best-known examples of these layered drinks is the Tequila Sunrise (*opposite*). Another example uses equal measures of grenadine, Parfait Amour (a violet liqueur) and Maraschino (a clear cherry liqueur). Pour in that order into a chilled wine glass, then place in the refrigerator until they separate.

SOME DRINK STYLES

Cocktail A mixed drink which incorporates a spirit or wine base with a modifier such as vermouth and extra flavouring such as sugar and bitters.

Cooler A refreshing long drink often made in large quantities as in Punch.

Collins A drink made with a base liquor, lemon juice and sugar.

Flip Any drink made with whole eggs.

Frappé A drink served over crushed ice, notably a liqueur.

Highball In the United States, this virtually means the same as Cocktail, but strictly speaking it refers to a drink made with two measures of spirit with ice and soda. It is served in a 10 fl. ounces (28 cl.) highball glass (tall tumbler).

Punch A drink made with a mixture of spirits and/or wines with added spices, fruit juices and sugar. May be served hot or cool.

Sour A cocktail made with a base spirit, a flavouring of liqueur and lemon juice, shaken with ice. A short drink served on the rocks or straight.

Toddy A traditional mixture of straight spirit and water, served warm.

DRINKS

WHISKIES

THE CHOICE OF STYLES

What is whisky? First of all, should it be spelled with an "e" or not? The answer to this really depends on whether you are talking about Scotch or Canadian types, which have no "e", or Irish and American types, which use the extra letter. But the differences go a lot deeper than a simple question of spelling.

All whiskes are made with grain spirit distilled from cereals such as barley and corn. But each country has evolved different styles, according to its popular taste. Apart from the four major producers already mentioned, Australia, New Zealand and Japan are also notable whiskey distilling nations.

SCOTCH WHISKY

There is one vital difference between styles of Scotch which needs to be understood. That is the distinction between a blend and a single malt. On the top shelf, it is quite easy to recognize which is which, since prices for any single malt are invariably higher than those for a blend. But there is a third category: the deluxe blend. Especially favoured in the United States, these whiskies from Scotland are often presented in very attractive bottles and packages. Indeed, as exporting is the mainstay of the Scotch industry, great pains are taken to present the product as pleasingly as possible. Apart from price, how do you choose the Scotch you need for a certain purpose? The following guide should make your decision easy.

SCOTCH BLENDS

The great majority of Scotch whiskies on sale are blends. As the name implies, each bottle contains a special blend of various whiskies which are selected according to the house style of a particular producer. Consistency is the keynote, so that the consumer can safely buy a favourite brand again and again and know it will always taste just the same. Although this type of Scotch is today's preferred bottle, it has only been available for about 100 years. It was introduced to rival French brandy, a favourite base for mixing with soda as a long drink in the 19th century. When a disease wiped out many French vines, brandy production was affected, and the time was ripe for Scotland to offer an alternative. Blended Scotch is smooth and fairly light, with enough richness to mix well yet retain its distinctive flavour.

To achieve a desired taste, blenders mix whiskies made by the traditional pot still method, known as malts, and those made by modern continuous stills, known as grain whiskies. The grain whiskies have the required lightness and the small percentage of added malt gives that richness which makes one brand different from another.

THE CHOICE OF BLEND

Many well-known blended Scotches are owned and distributed by a single company, the Distillers Company Ltd (D.C.L.). Brands they promote include bestsellers such as *Johnny Walker, Haig, VAT 69, Dewar's White Label, Black & White,* and *White Horse.* All of these are similar in quality, with just enough malt to give extra flavour. The malt whisky comes from distilleries owned by the parent company. When it comes to choice of a bottle for your home bar, it pays to try several before settling on a style which suits your palate.

Apart from the brands made by D.C. L., there are many famous independent names, including *Bells* and *Teachers. Bells,* a top-selling brand on the British market, has a slightly sweet flavour, while *Teachers* has a more noticeable malt aroma than many blends. *Grants, Standfast* and *The Famous Grouse* are other traditional blends that are preferred by drinkers who like plenty of character in their Scotch.

For drinkers who favour a truly light flavour, and this applies to a great many Americans who like a long, cool drink without too rich a finish, there are various good quality brands. Two of the most renowed are *Cutty Sark* and *J & B Rare,* both shipped to the United States by old-fashioned English wine and spirit merchants.

For those who plan to use their Scotch blend in cocktails, which may have several other powerful ingredients, it is a good idea to buy one of the less expensive brands which are lower in alcohol. Most Scotch is sold in the United States at 86 proof, but some brands are only 80 proof. Examples include *Usher's Green Stripe, Passport* (from the giant House of Segram) and *King George,* as well as many of the house brands from supermarkets and off-licences.

DELUXE BLENDS

Many familiar names in the world of Scotch appear in two guises: the basic bottle and deluxe version. For instance, *Johnnie Walker* has a *Red Label* and a more expensive connoisseur's *Black Label.* Why the two styles? Essentially, a deluxe blend contains a higher proportion of the more expensive malts than the inexpensive grain whiskies. They are fuller in flavour and often higher in strength – at least 86 proof. If there is a specified age on the label, it means that the youngest of the whiskies used in the blend is at least that old, be it 8, 10, 12 or 25 years.

These blends are meant to be offered simply to show off their refined flavour. Ice and water, or club soda, are the usual mixers. In Britain they would be served neat, without ice, in a traditional tumbler. Some are described as "liqueur Scotch," a term which simply means that they are ideal after-dinner drinks. Unlike true liqueurs, however, they are not sweetened or "concocted" in any way.

DELUXE BRANDS

These whiskies are meant to appeal to the eyes as well as the palate. They are packaged in attractive boxes and bottles and make good gifts; some are sold in crystal decanters for an opulent offering. Famous names include *Johnnie Walker Black Label; Old Parr; Ballantine's; Chiva Regal;* and *The Antiquary. Haig* also market a deluxe blend in the distinctive "dimple" squat bottle. And *John O'Groats* whisky is from the company which also makes *Drambuie,* a Scotch-based liqueur.

Straight malt whisky

SCOTCH MALT WHISKIES

Here are the classics of Scotland, drinks for the connoisseur. The pungent flavour of a traditional Scotch malt whisky takes some time to get used to, especially for anyone whose taste tends to the lighter side of drinking. But once you get to know the smoky aromas of these unusual whiskies they can grow on you. Only tiny quantities are available when compared to the output of blended Scotch, and a good deal of the malt distilled in the Scottish Highlands goes to be blended and add character to a lighter bottling.

What is malt whisky? It is the forerunner of modern, lighter versions, made in a pot still, and using a "beer" fermented from malted barley. The process is long and complex and involves two distillations in the attractive rounded copper stills. This is the way spirits were made before the 19th century, and today only top-quality Scotch, French cognac, Irish whiskey, and a few special vats in other countries are prepared this way.

As so much care must go into the making of these whiskies, they tend to cost far more than the blends. In addition, they are all aged in wood casks for at least eight years before they are bottled. Some are far older, and consequently smoother. To confuse the issue, there are now also some blended malts on the market, also known as vatted malts. Where most malt whisky is from a single distillery, these are produced by blending various malts, perhaps all owned by a larger company. However, there is no grain whisky in the blend.

THE CHOICE OF MALTS

Classic malts are many and varied, and your personal taste should be the deciding factor. If you want to experiment, try a bottle of any of the following and you can be sure of a pleasant glassful: *The Balvenie*; *Cardhu* (owned by Johnnie Walker); *Glenfiddich*, a popular brand in duty-free shops worldwide; *The Glenlivet*, Scotland's original distillery and some say still the best; *Glenmorangie*, a lighter malt with delicate flavour; *The Macallan*, favoured by the experts; *Tomatin*, from the Highlands' largest distillery.

As a contrast to these elegant Highland malts, try a bottle from the islands off Scotland. Both Islay and Skye produce some of the finer malts, renowed for an incomparable fullness and richness of flavour. Examples include *Bowmore, Lagavulin* and *Laphroaig* from Islay; and *Talisker* from the Isle of Skye, where Bonnie Prince Charlie sheltered from the English during his bid for the throne.

SERVING MALTS

Normally these fine and rare whiskies are served alone, without any addition. But in a warmer climate it is often essential to add ice. Lovers of malt are convinced that only real Highland Spring Water may be added without changing the flavour of their favourite drink, but any still or sparkling mineral water is appropriate. Like the deluxe blends, these are ideal after-dinner drinks.

As a good range of deluxe blends and single malts are available in duty-free shops, they make excellent gifts to bring to friends when returning from holidays abroad.

IRISH WHISKEY

When it comes to flavour, Irish whiskey is quite readily distinguished from Scotch. The makers claim all manner of mysterious reasons why this should be so, but in reality it seems that climatic conditions are an important factor, and the fact that Irish whiskey is distilled not twice, but three times. This appears to give additional smoothness to the finished spirit. Like Scotch, Irish whiskey is aged in wood casks for at least three years before bottling.

THE CHOICE OF BRANDS

All Irish whiskies are controlled by a single company – the Irish Distillers Group. There are sixteen different labels to choose from, all with varying characteristics. American tastes seem to run to a "fruity" style of whiskey, with some sweetness, so preferred brands in the U.S. include *Murphy's, Jameson*, and *Power's Gold Label*. In Ireland, it is said that the Catholics drink Power's, and Protestants prefer Jameson's. So bear that in mind the next time you're entertaining Irish friends!

From Northern Ireland comes *Old Bushmills*, equivalent in style to a Scotch single malt. Like its Scottish rivals, this whiskey tends to be very heavy and rich in flavour. This particular company also sells a deluxe brand, known as *Old Bushmills Black Bush*.

For a really authentic taste of old Ireland, try a glass of *Paddy*, a local favourite with a rather sharp style.

SERVING IRISH WHISKEY

Irish Coffee is the obvious choice as this smooth whiskey blends perfectly with dark coffee. Simply pour one jigger of Irish whiskey into a freshly-brewed cup of strong coffee, add to sugar to taste, then stir. The final touch is a generous dash of heavy cream which should be allowed to float on the surface of the coffee, where it makes an attractive swirling pattern. Or the really indulgent can choose whipped cream – not for dieters.

In Ireland, Irish whiskey would be served either in coffee, or simply alone – straight in a short tumbler. Add ice if preferred.

CANADIAN WHISKY

This is the mixing whisky *par excellence*. Like Scotch, it has no "e" in the spelling, and this is due to Canada's early links with Scotland. Canadian whisky is often called rye, to distinguish it from bourbon, a specifically American drink. However, rye whiskey is also made in the

United States, so the name can be confusing.

In fact, Canadian whisky is made chiefly of corn, with some rye and barley. The exact proportions are a secret known only to the individual blenders, but there are usually about seven parts of corn to one of rye. The whisky is made in a continuous still to give a light, delicate spirit. This is aged in wood casks for at least three years before bottling. Before sale, a little pure rye (100 per cent) is often added, together with some caramel to give extra colour. However, a pale colour is typical of Canadian whisky and considered a very desirable feature.

THE CHOICE OF BRANDS

The giant Seagram Company dominates the Canadian whisky scene, and is also active in the United States. In fact, a great quantity of the whisky made in Canada is exported to the United States by this company and other multi-national groups such as Hiram Walker.

Choosing a brand to suit your taste should not prove difficult. All Canadian whisky is light and agreeable – ideal in fact for the habitual "white spirit" drinker who normally prefers vodka or white rum. Top selling brands include *Seagram's V.O.* (meaning Very Old); *Canadian Club* from Hirman Walker; *Black Velvet*, promoted by the Heublein Corporation; *Windsor Supreme* from National Distillers; and *Canadian Mist*. Also under the umbrella of the Segram organization are those whiskies called *Calvert*, including the fine and rare *Calvert Masterpiece*, and *Canadian Lord Calvert* which is sent to the U.S. for bottling to reduce tax costs.

The majority of these whiskies are sold at about 80 proof, but some special bottlings are up to 86.8. These tend to be older blends, and consequently more expensive.

SERVING CANADIAN WHISKY

Unlike Scotch, which is very often served straight or with water only, this whisky is meant to be offered in a mixed drink. Apart from the many uses in cocktails good mixers include mineral water, ginger ale and other sodas such as lemon-lime, or even cola. Use the classic short whisky tumbler for all these drinks, with plenty of ice.

Canadian whisky with dry ginger

Bourbon on the rocks

AMERICAN WHISKEY

Whiskey-making in the United States dates back to the earliest Colonial days. The first bottles were rough "moonshine" and as late as 1871, most whiskey was sold direct from the cask into the customer's own flask.

In the 18th century both Scottish and Irish settlers came to the New World bringing with them the expert knowledge of whiskey-making which was to lead to the setting-up of a great American industry. At first, distillers were able to make as much whiskey as they wished without government interference. But this happy state did not last long and soon the tax collectors were out gathering funds from this activity for Washington. This caused many east coast distillers to move inland, notably to Kentucky, to establish their business beyond the tax collector's reach. From these beginnings came the early Kentucky bourbon whiskies. Bourbon is one of the counties of Kentucky where a certain Reverend Elijah Craig is said to have made the first true whiskey of this type in 1789. His secret was the use of charred-oak barrels, still favoured to this day.

STYLES OF AMERICAN WHISKEY

The story of American whiskies is almost as difficult as Scotch for the consumer. Basically, there are three major styles: straights, blends and light whiskies. This last category is rare today, but a few years ago light whiskies were heavily promoted as the drink for those wanting an alternative to vodka and white rum. Overall, by far the largest share of the market is taken up by blends, which are invariably less expensive. As in Scotland, a blend is made of a number of straight whiskies mixed in order to retain a certain style which is associated with the label.

Bourbon and rye are the two most notable straight whiskies, although it is also possible to find straight corn. The description depends on the particular mix of grain in the original "mash" which goes into distillation. Bourbon contains at least 51 per cent corn, while rye must include a similar proportion of rye in the mash. Both bourbon and rye are aged in charred oak barrels to give a smoky flavour.

THE CHOICE OF BRANDS

Blends must include at least 20 per cent by volume of 100 proof straight whiskey to ensure a certain minimum quality standard. These bottles are the perfect basis for mixing cocktails. Brands include all those sold as "in-house" brands in supermarkets and off-licences, as well as famous names like *Seagram's 7 Crown*, which is the world's best-selling whiskey.

Straight whiskies have been aged in oak for at least two years and are sold at between 80 and 110 proof. Each straight whiskey comes from a single distillery and no other whiskey may be added.

Bourbon whiskey is a customer favourite with its distinctive flavour and full style. Most good-quality bourbons are aged for at least four years before bottling. Only whiskey made in the U.S. may be called bourbon and it is generally agreed that the best bourbons come from Kentucky. Kentucky bourbons must spend at least one year aging in Kentucky. A bourbon need not always be a straight whiskey, although these are preferred by whiskey connoisseurs. Blended bourbons are also popular. While blended bourbons are commonly sold at around U.S. 80 proof, straight whiskeys are often around 86 proof, or even up to 101 proof.

Wild Turkey is a well-known Kentucky straight bourbon which is sold at 101 proof. It is meant to be served straight, like the single malts of Scotland. Other premium bourbons include *Old Grand-Dad, Old Forester* and *I.W. Harper*. Among the bourbons sold at 80 proof are *Old Crow, Early Times* and *Ten High*. These and other familiar brands are ideal for making Mint Juleps and other traditional bourbon-based cocktails.

TENNESSEE WHISKEY

This rather special American whiskey tends to sell at premium prices, but there is a good reason for this. The spirit is filtered through charcoal made from sugar-maple trees before going into charred oak barrels for aging. The filtering is done slowly and is said to give a particular flavour. In addition to this feature, many Tennessee whiskies are also sour mash. This means that a special yeast is used in making the original "beer" which goes for distillation into whiskey, giving the whiskey a certain tartness favoured by those who appreciate good whiskey.

The most renowned name in Tennessee whiskey-making is *Jack Daniel*, who founded his distillery in Lynchburg to make use of his discoveries about the charcoal filtration process. The label usually found is black and the whiskey in the bottle is at least five years old. Other Tennessee whiskies are *Ezra Brooks* and *George A. Dickel*.

SERVING AMERICAN WHISKEY

Blended bourbons or brands like *Seagram's 7 Crown* are ideal for cocktail use. Serve straight bourbons over ice or with a little water.

JAPANESE WHISKEY

The Japanese have long enjoyed the flavour of whiskey, and since the 1940s have been making their own version with increasing success. *Suntory* is the principal label, and their best bottles such as *The Whisky* have a proportion of imported Scotch malt in the blend. These whiskies are available in the U.S. under labels including *Signature* and *Excellence*. The other major Japanese brand is *Nikka*.

AUSTRALIAN & NEW ZEALAND WHISKIES

These closely resemble Scotch whisky in style, though they are a little softer. Well-known brands include *Bond 7* and *Corio*. Whisky has only been made in New Zealand for some 15 years, mainly by the *Wilson Distillers Company*.

SCOTCH WHISKY COCKTAILS

ROB ROY

☆ ☆ ☆

2 measures Scotch whisky
1 measure sweet vermouth
1 dash Angostura bitters

Pour all ingredients into a tumbler to mix, and stir well with ice. Then strain into a cocktail glass; garnish with a cocktail cherry.
Note: This is a version of the classic Manhattan made with Scotch.

BOBBY BURNS

☆ ☆

1 measure Scotch whisky
1 measure sweet vermouth
3 dashes of Benedictine liqueur

Place ice cubes in shaker and shake all ingredients well. Strain into a cocktail glass and decorate with a twist of orange peel.
Note: This subtly-flavoured drink is named after Robert Burns, Scotland's finest poet.

WHISKY SOUR

☆ ☆

2 measures Scotch whisky
1 ½ teaspoons sugar (or sugar
  syrup)
Juice ½ lemon
Soda water to taste
Egg white (optional)

Place ice cubes in shaker then
add whisky, sugar, lemon juice
and egg white (optional, it gives
the drink a frothy appearance).
Shake well then strain into a short
tumbler. Add soda water to taste.
Note: If a short drink is preferred,
this may be served in a cocktail
glass without the soda water.
Garnish with a slice of orange if
desired.

RUSTY NAIL

☆ ☆

1 measure Scotch whisky
1 measure Drambuie

Place ice cubes in a tumbler then
add ingredients and stir gently.
Strain into a cocktail glass and
serve. *Note:* In Britain this drink
would be prepared without ice
and served at room temperature.

35

BRAINSTORM

 ☆ ☆

1 measure Irish whiskey
2 dashes dry vermouth
2 dashes Benedictine

Stir all ingredients in a tumbler or jug, then strain into a cocktail glass. Decorate with a twist of orange peel.

BLUE BLAZER

☆ ☆

2 measures Irish whiskey
1 measure clear honey
½ measure lemon juice
2-3 measures water
Cinnamon sticks (garnish)

Pour all ingredients into a pan and heat very gently until the honey has dissolved. Place a teaspoon into a short tumbler and pour drink carefully into the glass (the spoon prevents the glass cracking). Serve with cinnamon sticks. *Note:* This is a marvellous therapy for the common cold, and also a delightful warming drink for winter days.

RATTLESNAKE

  ☆

1 measure Canadian whisky
½ egg white
½ measure lemon juice
Dash sugar syrup or ½ teaspoon sugar
1 dash Pernod

Put all ingredients into the blender with some cracked ice. Blend until smooth, then strain into cocktail glass. *Note:* This drink is often best made in larger amounts for several people. Simply multiply the ingredients as required.

OLD FASHIONED

☆ ☆

2 measures Canadian whisky
1 sugar lump
2 dashes Angostura bitters
Twist of lemon peel

Put the sugar lump into a small tumbler then add the bitters. Allow to soak in, then crush the sugar with a spoon. Add a little ice, the twist of lemon peel and a slice of orange. Pour on the whisky and stir well.

MANHATTAN

2 measures bourbon or rye
   whiskey
1 measure sweet vermouth
1 dash Angostura bitters

Place ice cubes in shaker then
add all ingredients and shake
well. Strain into a cocktail glass.
Note: This drink may also be
made with Canadian whisky for a
lighter taste.

DRY MANHATTAN
Make as a Manhattan but
substituting dry vermouth for
sweet vermouth.

COWBOY

2 measures American whiskey
1 measure double cream
Sprinkle nutmeg

Put cracked ice in shaker then
add ingredients (except nutmeg)
and shake well – strain into a wine
glass and then sprinkle on
nutmeg to taste. Serve at once.

WHISKEY HIGHBALL

2 measures whiskey
Juice of ½ lemon
Soda water to top up

Fill a tall tumbler with crushed ice
and add whiskey and lemon
juice. Top with soda water – a
very refreshing sharp drink.
Decorate with lemon slice if
desired.

FRUIT SOUR

1 measure Scotch or bourbon
1 measure lemon juice
1 measure fruit liqueur of choice

Shake well with ice and pour into
a rocks glass. Generally served
on the rocks and decorated with
a slice of orange, a maraschino
cherry and two short thin straws.

EARTHQUAKE

☆ ☆ ☆

1 measure whiskey
1 measure gin
1 measure Pernod

Place ice cubes in shaker, then
add all ingredients and shake
well. Strain into a cocktail glass.
Note: not for the occasional
drinker!

BOURBON SOUR

☆

1 measure bourbon
2 tablespoons lemon juice
2 teaspoons sugar syrup

Mix with ice in shaker, strain into
glass, add soda to taste.
Decorate with lemon slice if
desired.

WHISKEY FIX

☆ ☆

2 measures whiskey
Juice of ½ lemon
1 teaspoon castor sugar

Shake lemon and sugar with ice and strain into highball glass. Fill glass with ice. Add whiskey, stir and add slice of lemon.

MINT JULEP

☆ ☆

2 measures bourbon
1 teaspoon castor sugar
Sprig of fresh mint
Soda to top up

Put the sugar, mint and a little soda into a tall tumbler. Mash these together to release mint flavour. Add the bourbon and then top with soda to taste.

41

VODKA

Vodka is a modern success story in the drinks world. Of course, it has been a favourite of Eastern Europeans for many centuries, but it is only in the past 30 years that vodka has become popular in the West as well. The name means simply "water" in Russian, a reference to the belief that all spirits are the water of life – *zhiznennia voda* in Russia, *eau de vie* in France.

In its home lands, which extend from Russia to Poland and Germany, this colourless spirit is usually served ice-cold in tiny glasses. The idea is to drink it in a single gulp, often accompanied by a glass of lager beer and a selection of smoked foods. True enthusiasts in the United States and western Europe also savour vodka this way, but in the main it is an incomparable base for mixed drinks.

As vodka has only the most delicate of flavours, and almost no after-taste (it "leaves you breathless" in the words of a famous Smirnoff advertising campaign) it will mix readily with any other drink, from apple juice to beef consommé. And new ideas for mixed vodka drinks are dreamed up almost daily.

Smirnoff is perhaps the most celebrated name in vodka circles. The original family members were privileged courtiers in Tsarist Russia. When the Revolution came they were naturally out of favour and fled to France, taking the secret of distilling their renowed vodkas with them. In Paris, Vladimir Smirnoff, head of the family, made contact with a Russian-born American named Rudolf Kunett, and by 1934 there was a distillery in Connecticut making vodka according to the traditional recipe. Demand was slow so Kunett sold out to the chairman of Heublein, then a local liquor business, but today one of the world's leading corporate liquor traders. Their position today is due in large part to the enormous worldwide sales of *Smirnoff* vodka.

The first vodka cocktail to gain popularity in the United States was a curious blend – vodka with ginger ale. It was a case of necessity being the mother of invention, when a bartender in Los Angeles found himself hopelessly overstocked with both drinks. In the Cold War climate of the late-1940s he coined the name **Moscow Mule** to describe the mixture and the idea spread like wildfire. Following this example, new blends were created to promote the growing sales, with drinks like the **Bullshot** and the **Bloody Mary** proving lasting favourites for serving at all times of the day.

Screwdriver

Vodka has a reputation for keeping hangovers at bay, and of course the manufacturers do nothing to harm this image. However, it is not literally true. What is indisputable is that since this is the least flavoured of all spirits, and because it is filtered many times through charcoal before bottling, it has none of the congeners which arise during distillation and lend both Scotch and cognac their distinctive pungency. The presence of congeners in alcoholic beverages is thought to produce hangovers.

The opposite problem arises when vodka disappears into a cocktail. It is very popular with younger drinkers and occasional drinkers because it does not give a drink a "spiritous" taste. But this means it is hard to evaluate how strong the drink is. So beware – don't spoil your party by this miscalculation. Check our star ratings when preparing cocktails to work out relative strengths of vodka-mixed drinks.

Although vodka appears to be such a neutral spirit, there are remarkable differences between brands. The "true" vodkas and schnapps of Eastern Europe tend to have more flavour and higher alcoholic strength than the Western versions. As a rule of thumb, reserve imported vodkas for drinking straight, and domestic bottles for cocktails.

THE CHOICE OF BRANDS

Selecting a vodka from the shelf can be confusing because all the Western brands make strenuous efforts to look as Russian as possible. Crests abound and most of the titles are decidely Tsarist in style. Apart from the small print on the label giving the country of origin, there are two other clues to help you choose. First of all, check the alcoholic strength. An authentic Russian or Polish vodka will tend to be bottled at around 86 to 114 proof, although stronger versions exist. Domestic U.S. or British-made vodkas will average about 80 proof.

Secondly, take a look at the price. A higher price tag is a sure indication of an import! Not that all domestic vodkas are similarly priced. Like whiskies, there is a full range of styles available, including premium higher-strength brands.

Smirnoff, as already mentioned, has become a household word wherever vodka is known. It is distilled under license from Heublein in many countries. The most important styles of Smirnoff to remember are the red label at 80 U.S. proof, the silver label at 90 and the blue at 100 proof.

Other leading brands on the U.S. domestic market include *Popov*, a less expensive vodka made by Heublein; *Kamchatka*, another top value brand, from the National Distillers group; *Schenleys*, *Fleischmann's*, *Hiram Walker* and *Mr. Boston*, all from the well-known liquor concerns. Most of these represent excellent value. *Seagram*, the world's largest liquor company, are also active in vodka production. *Wolfschmidt* is a premium brand, recommended for drinking straight; other brands include *Crown Russe* and *Nicolai*.

In Britain, favourite brands include the various *Smirnoff* lables, made under license by Gilbeys, and *Vladivar*, made in Warrington, Lancashire, despite its Russian-style label. *Gordon's* and *Gilbey's* own vodkas are also made in Britain. These are mainly intended for export, and a great deal is sold in the United States. In Britain, these two companies are best-known for their gin. In fact, the distillation of vodka and that of gin are very similar processes.

VODKAS OF EASTERN EUROPE

Polish vodka is renowned for its strength and in the United States powerful Polish spirit is often purchased to add extra "punch" to a fruit and wine concoction at parties. Known as *Polish Pure Spirit*, this is bottled at 114 proof, and was once intended for use on long journeys in sub-zero conditions in Poland, when even spirit would freeze if it were less than 100 proof.

But not all Polish vodka is as strong. There are many different labels which have distinctive flavours. Unlike domestic bottlings, which strive toward a neutral style, the imported Polish versions aim for individuality. So the flavour of sugarbeet or rye which went into the "mash" for distillation is still detectable. In addition, there are many vodkas which have extra flavouring, including *Zubrowka*, which is bottled with blades of grass from a park where rare bison graze. *Starka*, a golden-coloured vodka has Spanish Malaga wine blended in

45

to accentuate the rye base flavour. Other flavours available include rowan, juniper and cherry.

This enthusiasm for flavoured vodkas has led some U.S. companies to follow suit, and mint, orange, lime and cherry flavours may be found in U.S. bottlings.

Finnish vodka is exported under the *Finlandia* label and bottled in a distinctive stippled square-shouldered bottle. It has a "western" taste.

Russian vodka may also be up to 114 proof, but the average strength found on the export market is lower. Look for *Stolichnaya* and *Moskovskaya* labels if you want to try a typical brand. For a real Russan touch, add some black pepper to your glass of vodka – a favourite toast of Peter the Great. In Russia, this blend is even sold ready-mixed, as *Pertsovka* vodka.

In Scandinavia the favoured spirit is *akvavit* or *aquavit*, which closely resembles vodka and is commonly served straight, ice-cold in the style of Eastern European vodkas. The Danes are especially fond of this powerful eye-opener with their meals, particularly *smorgasbord*. Many interesting flavours are available, including cardamom, caraway and anise. Look for the name *Aalborg* on the label for a true Danish aquavit, as this firm makes 90 percent of Danish aquavit. Apart from the standard clear vodka-type spirit, there are also golden-toned aquavits, including *Aalborg Jubilaeums*, flavoured with dill and coriander, and Norwegian *Linie Aquavit*, which is shipped in wood casks on a long voyage to Australia and back, so that the spirit takes on the warm colour and flavour of the wood.

The Germans also enjoy their own version of vodka, notably in the Northern regions. The word *schnapps* is used in Germany to mean any strong spirit, and they generally drink schnapps straight and well-chilled. However, it may be flavoured to resemble gin or even rye whiskey. These flavoured styles are also known as Korn. A good example is *Doornkaat*, which is distilled three times for extra smoothness. *Furst Bismarck* is a favourite brand in Germany – this schnapps is aged in ash wood casks. Schnapps is also produced in the United States, but it is generally sweetened and flavoured so that it becomes a liqueur rather than a straight spirit.

HOW TO SERVE VODKA

All these rather neutral "white spirits" lend themselves to any style of drink. If you are hesitant to try vodka, just experiment around drinks you already enjoy. Make a dry Martini with vodka, or mix it with tonic as a long drink. If you like your whiskey straight, then sample an ice-cold glass of vodka for a change.

Serving vodka straight

In Tsarist Russia, special vodka glasses were manufactured with very fragile stems, so the stems could be snapped in an extravagant gesture after toasting the Tsar. Occasionally, glasses were even hurled into the fireplace after drinking. In our more practical age, such theatrics seem excessive, so to try vodka in truly Russian style, simply select small wine or cocktail glasses with stems and chill them in the refrigerator or freezer for about one hour before use. The vodka should also be placed in the freezer to give it the attractive viscosity in the glass which is sought by lovers of this fiery drink.

One spectacular notion for use when an Eastern European party is planned would be to freeze a bottle of top-quality domestic or imported vodka inside a block of ice. Serve caviar with it in a silver bowl over lots of crushed ice. If caviar is outside your price range, try smoked herring or other fish or smoked sausage. Spicy sausage is especially good with the flavoured vodkas and schnapps.

If not Eastern Europe, how about Denmark as a theme for entertaining? Their *smorgasbord* is a wonderful way to offer plenty to eat in a simple fashion. Offer a range of rye and wheat bread with smoked fish.

Cheeses, cold meats and cool lager beer complete the picture. Offer *aquavit* to your guests in small, well-chilled glasses.

Normally, vodka and other similar spirits are served without ice, but there is no reason why you should not pour it over a few cubes in a short tumbler if your prefer.

After a meal, the French have adopted a Russian habit which is a pleasant alternative to liqueurs or brandy. If you have just finished a cup of black coffee, simply pour a single measure of vodka into the empty cup and let it mingle with the coffee aroma which remains. Then drink it off in one gulp – a truly refreshing end to a meal, especially for those who find other drinks too sweet.

In Scandinavia, they place silver coins in the base of a coffee cup, then pour in coffee until they disappear from sight. Vodka is then added (usually *aquavit*) until the coin reappears. This makes a warming drink on a winter's night, with less calories than Irish coffee with cream.

Vodka and tonic

From the hundreds of cocktails invented to exploit vodka's unique versatility as a mixer, here are a few classics to sample at home:

VODKA MARTINI

Also known as a **Vodkatini**, this alternative to the traditional Martini is associated with James Bond. A connection with glamorous overtones. As with the gin Martini, this cocktail may be shaken or stirred according to preference.

3 measures vodka
1 measure dry white vermouth

The purist's way of making the cocktail is to place 4-5 ice cubes into a large mixing glass, then pour in the vodka and vermouth. Stir gently and before the ice begins to melt, strain into a chilled cocktail glass with a stem. Garnish with a twist of lemon peel.

If a shaker is preferred, simply pour the ingredients over ice cubes in your shaker; shake well, then strain and serve. The appearance of a shaken cocktail is supposed to be less crystalline that that of the stirred drink — judge for yourself.

BLOODY MARY

 ☆

1 measure vodka
2 measures tomato juice
1/3 measure lemon juice
1 dash Worcestershire sauce
Salt and pepper to taste

This is renowned as an "eye opener" for those not at their best in the morning. It makes an excellent brunch drink as well as a refreshing cocktail before eating.

Shake all the ingredients well together with a few ice cubes, then strain into a tall tumbler or wine glass. Garnish with a celery stick which has a few leaves. Add salt, celery salt or black pepper to taste as you serve. If preferred, this drink may be served over crushed ice.

For a **Bloody Caesar** use Clamato juice (clam juice with tomatoes) in place of the tomato for an unusual seafood cocktail in a glass. Add Tabasco for extra punch.

This recipe may also be used with tequila to make a **Bloody Maria.**

BLACK RUSSIAN

 ☆ ☆ ☆

2 measures vodka
1 measure Kahlua coffee liqueur
Cola (optional)

Simply pour the vodka, then the Kahlua over ice cubes in a chilled tumbler. If desired, add some cola to make a longer drink – this is served in a tall tumbler. Stir.

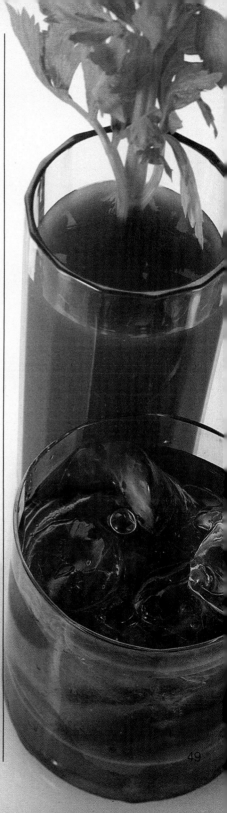

HARVEY WALLBANGER

 ☆ ☆

1 measure vodka
½ measure Galliano liqueur
4 measures orange juice

This drink is named after a
Californian sportsman who
created the blend to drown his
sorrows after losing a match; he
was left feeling so relaxed that he
collided with the wall, hence the
title Harvey Wallbanger. It is very
easy to drink, as are all cocktails
made with fruit juice – so beware!

Fill a tall tumbler with ice
cubes or crushed ice, then pour
over the vodka, followed by the
orange juice. Pour the Galliano
carefully over the back of a spoon
so that it floats on the surface of
the drink. Garnish with a slice of
orange and a cocktail cherry, if
desired.

WHITE RUSSIAN

☆ ☆ ☆

2 measures vodka
1 measure Kahlua
Double cream

Pour over ice as for **Black
Russian**, then carefully add thick
cream over the back of a spoon
to create an attractive "layered"
effect.

SCREWDRIVER

 ☆ ☆

3 measures vodka
Orange juice to taste
Sliced oranges (garnish)

Choose a tall or short tumbler
according to strength required.
Fill with ice cubes or crushed ice
then pour over vodka, followed
by orange juice. Stir well, and
decorate with orange slices.

MOSCOW MULE

(or SMIRNOFF MULE)

 ☆

1 ½ measures vodka
Ginger ale to taste (or lemon/lime
    soda for **Smirnoff Mule**)
Juice of ½ lime
Twist of lime peel
Sliced lime (garnish)

Pour the lime juice into a tall
tumbler then drop in the twist of
peel. Add ice cubes, then vodka.
Top with ginger ale or soda.
Decorate with sliced lime.

GIMLET

1 ½ measures vodka
1 measure Rose's lime juice or
    fresh lime juice
1 teaspoon castor sugar
Sliced lime (garnish)

Place about 5 ice cubes in shaker
then add vodka, sugar and lime
juice. Shake well and strain into a
cocktail glass, previously chilled.
Decorate with lime slices.

VODKA COLLINS

2 measures vodka
Juice of ½ lime
1 teaspoon castor sugar
Soda water to taste
Lime slices and cocktail cherry
    (garnish)

Place about 5 ice cubes in
shaker, then add vodka, and lime
juice. Shake well, and strain into a
tall tumbler. If desired, fill the
tumbler with crushed ice; or add
ice cubes. Decorate with lime
slices and a cocktail cherry.

BULLSHOT

☆

1 measure vodka
3 measures beef consommé
Dash Worcestershire sauce
Lemon juice to taste
Black pepper
Celery (garnish)

Place ice cubes in a mixing glass, then pour in the vodka, beef consommé and dash of Worcestershire sauce. Stir well, then pour carefully into a short tumbler. Add lemon juice and black pepper to taste. Decorate with a stick of celery.

KATINKA

☆ ☆ ☆

1½ measures vodka
1 measure apricot brandy
½ measure lime juice

Pour all ingredients into shaker over ice cubes. Shake well. Then strain into a cocktail glass previously filled with crushed ice.

GIN

It can be argued that if you only chose one spirit for your home cocktail bar, it should be gin. Gin has a fragrance and subtle taste which makes it perfect for mixing. And, of course, for drinking straight. Choose a genever gin from Holland or perhaps a Plymouth gin from Britain for this style of drink. Some may argue that the Dry Martini is really nothing more than a chilled glass of straight gin, but purists would shudder at this misunderstanding and mention the difficulty of mixing "the real Martini."

Yet gin was not always a cocktail ingredient. Time was when it was most commonly offered warm, often with water added. Nor was gin always "dry." Until only about 50 years ago, the sweetened styles of gin were best sellers worldwide. Even today, sweet gins are still sold, sometimes with added flavours such as lemon.

Most experts agree that gin was invented by the Dutch. A Dr. Sylvius of the University of Leyden created a blend of pure spirit with added juniper flavouring for use as a medicine to aid digestion. Of course, this was not the first time spirits had been proposed as a medicine. Since Roman times distilled beverages have been used to purify water and settle upset stomachs, even to soothe pain during operations and childbirth. But the taste of this juniper spirit also caught on as an everyday drink.

The French word for juniper is *genièvre*, so the Dutch called the drink *genever*, a name which persists to this day. The fashion for gin drinking spread to Britain during the 17th century, when King William III of Orange, born in Holland, came to the throne. The British called it *Hollands* after its country of origin, or gin as an abbreviation of the Dutch name *genever*.

The gin-drinking habit soon spread, and unfortunately its popularity was exploited by illicit distillers who added poisonous substances such as turpentine to their blends, thereby making it more economical to produce. This gin was sold very cheaply and it soon became a drink for the poor, who were naturally tempted to "drown their sorrows." The results are shown in the appalling visions of the artist, William Hogarth's Gin Lane, where both men and women lie drunk in the gutter.

In the United States gin was also a favoured drink during the 18th century due to British influence, and it began to be made there by both Dutch and British settlers at an early date. According to legend, Paul Revere and Sam Adams enjoyed cold gin with their dinner in Boston,

and even George Washington himself was known to partake of the occasional glass of gin and water. Farther south, the planters of Virginia enjoyed gin before going out foxhunting in true British style.

Once the production of gin was regulated during the 19th century in Britain, the drink became a favourite with the upper classes and was considered respectable even for women. Beautiful "gin palaces" were built to attract less affluent drinkers, complete with marble fittings and crystal chandeliers. Warm gin with water was the standard drink, as well as hot "toddies" and rum punches. A toddy included sugar and lemon juice as well as a good measure of sweet gin. This was a favourite with the many ladies who ventured out unaccompanied to these smart drinking establishments.

Gin's most glamorous period was undoubtedly the 1920s and 30s, when the Cocktail Era meant the creation of elegant mixed drinks based on this adaptable spirit. Ironically, it was Prohibition which brought about the refinement of the cocktail, as the "bathtub gin" of the speakeasies needed a lot of added flavour to disguise its rough qualities. Exotically-named drinks like Blue Moon and Pink Lady were fashionable with the Bright Young Things of the period.

GIN TODAY
What is gin? Basically, it is a pure clear spirit made in the modern continuous still, usually from grains including corn. At this stage gin has no flavour. The elusive taste of bottled gin comes from carefully blended additives; all of them natural flavours of plant origin, known in the business as "botanicals." The most important of these is still juniper, from the berries of that tree. Other much-used plants include coriander, also used in curry, angelica, for a slightly "earthy" taste, and cinnamon with dried orange. The precise blend of these aromatic ingredients depends on the style of each gin manufacturer, although juniper always predominates.

LONDON DRY GIN

This style of gin came about after the development of the continuous still in the 19th century. Prior to this, the old-fashioned pot still yielded a spirit with a great quantity of impurities – hence the horrors of Gin Lane associated with cheap gin. Spirits which have not been properly monitored during manufacture can be poisonous, because the first spirit to be vapourised during distillation is methyl alcohol or "meths." This is always discarded in the making of quality spirits for consumption, but before the invention of the continuous still this could not be done automatically.

So London, infamous in the 18th century for the deadly drink of Gin Lane, became in the 19th century a centre for the production of gin made to the highest standards. And the association has remained, although the name London Dry Gin no longer means that the gin is actually made in Britain at all.

When buying gin abroad, check the label of any bottle you intend to buy. There are three categories of gin which are labelled this way – the "real" gin of London which has been exported, and tends to be expensive; gin which has been made under license from the British original; and straightforward copies of the London style made by any number of liquor companies, often sold under house brands.

Gin and tonic

A GUIDE TO THE GIN BRANDS

If you intend to serve a true Dry Martini, then select an authentic London Dry Gin. Here are a few suggestions:

BEEFEATER Chosen by many Martini enthusiasts as top for flavour, this brand has been made by the same family business in Britain since the 19th century. It is sold at 94.6 proof.

BOMBAY This premium gin is made to a recipe dating from 1761 by G. & J. Greenall Ltd. Gin was a popular drink in the hot climate of India, especially when served with tonic water, containing quinine, a preventative against malaria.

BOODLES Another traditional British brand, attractively presented.

BOOTH'S This firm is the oldest distiller in Britain. Its brands include *House of Lords*, and a lighter gin, *High & Dry*.

GILBEY'S A well-known name in the British wine and spirits world. The company has extensive interests in both the United States and Canada, and its gin is distilled under license in those countries.

GORDON'S During Prohibition, this gin was much in demand among the bootleggers. Unlike American products of the period, this London gin was guaranteed pure. This demand led to the establishment of a distillery for Gordon's in the United States. The original recipe is followed precisely, and the distinctive gin which results is sold in a clear glass bottle with a decorative label. Gordon's gin manufactured in Great Britain is sold in a green bottle to distinguish it from the export version. This is to prevent illegal exports by unauthorised shippers.

TANQUERAY Connected with *Gordon's*, this company is owned by the Distillers Company Ltd. who have vast interests in the Scotch whisky business. Gin under this label has a particularly full, smooth quality. Like the British *Gordon's*, it is distilled at Finsbury, London, once renowed as a therapeutic hot spring area.

U.S. BRANDS

Most domestic brands of gin sell at around 80 proof. This means that they are not too powerful, nor too pungent, which makes them ideal for a cocktail base. *Seagram's* have an important share of this market, with their *Barnett's White Satin* gin, which is produced in the United

States. They also manufacture gin under the *Seagram* label which does well in the United States and Canada. Other top U.S. brands include *Calvert's, Fleischmann's, Hiram Walker* and *Schenley* (this last is sold at 90 proof, but is very light in flavour).

Of course, the brand leaders on the U.S. market are *Gordon's* and *Gilbey's*, both of which are imported London recipes made under license in the United States.

DUTCH GIN

This is the choice for those who love the flavour of juniper berries. Their aroma is quite unmistakable in this original *genever* gin, which is still made in traditional pot stills which give it extra flavour. The old-fashioned distilling method means that congeners (elements of the basic ingredients) remain in the finished spirit.

There are two distinct styles of *genever* gin. *Oude Genever* (Old Genever) has an extra high proportion of *moutwijn*, pungent malty base spirit. *Jonge Genever* is a more popular and subtle drink.

The principal brands include *De Kuyper* (with its heart-shaped label), *Bols*, with attractive brown crock bottles, *Hasekamp* and *Kokma*. Some of these firms are located in Schiedam, centre of the gin industry in Holland since the 16th century.

OTHER EUROPEAN GINS

In Britain, there is another distinct type of gin made outside London. This is *Plymouth Gin*, once made by the Plymouth Brethren, an order of monks. It has close connections with the British Navy, as ship's doctors used to recommend the taking of alcoholic bitters, such as *Angostura*, as a preventative medicine. However, these were so unpalatable alone that gin was added to persuade sailors to drink it down. Hence the invention of **Pink Gin,** still a favourite of old sea dogs.

The Irish make their own gin, which, like Plymouth Gin, has a somewhat softer flavour than London Dry Gin. Both attribute this to the quality of the water in their areas. *Cork Dry Gin* is produced by the Cork Distilleries Company.

Northern Germany is the home of excellent gin, which is like a more fragrant version of Dutch *genever*. The best-known is *Steinhager* from Westphalia. It is usually bottled in earthenware crocks.

Both Belgium and Spain also make gin for domestic consumption.

GIN WORLDWIDE

Wherever the British Empire once held sway, gin is still a favourite drink, notably in Africa and India. In Australia and New Zealand, London Dry Gin is made under license by *Gilbey's* and *Gordon's*.

FLAVOURED GINS

In the past, flavouring was commonly added to gin, with orange and lemon being the favourites. *Gordon's* in Britain and *Mr Boston* in the United States still keep up this tradition, and the Dutch often mix in fruit flavours with their *genever*. Pineapple and mint flavours are also obtainable in the United States.

Sloe gin, the traditional "stirrup cup of old England" drunk before a hunt meeting, is not a true gin, but a cordial made by steeping sloe berries in spirit and added sweetening. Sloes are the fruit of the blackthorn, and in Britain the making of sloe gin at home, using purchased pure spirit, is popular.

THE DRY MARTINI

The word "dry" is so closely associated with gin, that many assume that the Dry Martini has existed for as long as London Dry Gin. Much argument has raged over its origins, but most now agree that it was probably invented by a bartender of Italian origins named Martini, at the Knickerbocker Hotel in New York, around 1915. Of course, the coincidence of name with one of the world's top-selling vermouths could also have some significance and some believe a clever salesman promoted the name and the drink. The original Martini recipe called for one-half dry gin and one-half dry vermouth. This proportion has changed over the decades. The traditional Maritini uses 3 parts gin to 1 of vermouth; the dry Martini, 5 to 1 and the extra dry Martini, much favoured in the United States, 8 to 1.

SERVING GIN

As already mentioned, gin is the perfect mixer. So ideal, that it is hard to imagine serving gin straight. Yet Dutch *genever* gin should be offered this way, and it does make an excellent "eye opener." Like many spirits, gin does appear to settle the digestion. Serve ice-cold in tiny glasses. Close relations to this original way of serving gin are the **Dry Martini** and **Pink Gin** (see *recipes*).

Straightforward mixers for gin include the classic Schweppes tonic water, served over ice in a short tumbler with a slice of lemon called a Gin and Tonic. A more modern version made is with 7-Up, or a similar lemon/lime soda. Lovers of gin's aromatic quality also enjoy it in a mixture similar to a Bloody Mary, with tomato juice and Worcestershire sauce. Gin marries well with most fruit juices including orange, grapefruit and lime.

To make your own version of the Victorians' **Gin Toddy,** simply pour a measure of gin into a tall tumbler. Add warm water, sugar and lemon juice to taste. Stir well and add a twist of lemon peel. Honey may be substituted for the sugar to make a delicious concoction believed to help cure the common cold, or at least help you forget the symptoms for a while.

MARTINI

Y ℓ OR ▯ ☆ ☆ ☆

3 measures London Dry Gin
Dash of dry vermouth
Twist of lemon peel or stuffed
  olive

Chill the gin, vermouth and
cocktail glass before preparation.
Carefully pour the gin into a
mixing glass over ice cubes, then
add a touch of vermouth to taste
and stir gently. Pour into the
cocktail glass and garnish with
the twist of lemon peel or olive. A
shaker *can* be used, but purists
claim that this "bruises the gin"
and spoils its taste.

GIBSON MARTINI

Y ℓ OR ▯ ☆ ☆ ☆

3 measures London Dry Gin
Dash of dry vermouth
Cocktail onion

Prepare as for **Dry Martini** but
garnish with cocktail onion.

GIN AND IT

2 measures London Dry Gin
1 measure sweet vermouth
Orange slice

Shake ingredients well with ice cubes in your shaker, then strain into a cocktail glass. Garnish with orange slice. This is a typical "ladies" drink of the 1930s. The "It" refers to Italian (sweet) rather than French (dry) vermouth. For a **Gin and French** substitute dry vermouth to make a less powerful version of the Dry Martini. Garnish with a lemon slice.

GIN FIZZ

1 measure London Dry Gin
1 measure lemon juice
1 teaspoon castor or powdered sugar
Egg white (optional)
Lemon slice (garnish)

Place ice cubes in blender and add gin, lemon juice and sugar. Blend for 10 seconds, then add egg white if desired (it adds extra firmness to the finished drink). Blend again for 5 seconds. Pour into a short tumbler and decorate with a lemon slice and straws.

TOM COLLINS

2 measures gin
Juice of 1 lemon
1½ teaspoons castor sugar
Soda water to taste
Lemon slices and cocktail cherry
(garnish)

Place several ice cubes in shaker, then pour in gin and lemon juice. Carefully add measured sugar, and shake well to ensure it is fully dissolved. Then strain into a tall tumbler over ice cubes or crushed ice. Top up with soda water to taste. Garnish with lemon slices and cocktail cherry.

JOHN COLLINS

2 measures Irish gin
(other ingredients as for Tom
Collins)

Prepare as for **Tom Collins.** The Irish gin gives a slightly softer taste; this may be made with U.S. domestic gin also, as it often has a slightly less dry finish.

RAMOS FIZZ

☆ ☆

1 measure London Dry Gin
1 measure lemon juice
1 measure yellow Chartreuse
1½ teaspoons castor sugar
Soda water to taste

Place all ingredients except soda water in shaker and shake well. Pour through strainer into short tumbler and top with a little soda. This makes a marvellous eye-opener for brunch! Decorate with lemon slice if desired.

WHITE LADY

☆ ☆

1 measure gin
½ measure Cointreau (or other orange liqueur)
½ measure lemon juice
Orange slice and cocktail cherry

Make sure you choose only the colourless orange liqueurs (often known as *Triple Sec*) for this drink. Place ice cubes in shaker then add all ingredients; shake well, then strain into a cocktail glass. Decorate with an orange slice and cocktail cherry on one toothpick.

SILVER STREAK

☆ ☆

1 measure London Dry Gin
1 measure Kummel

This drink demands top quality gin which will balance the powerful caraway aroma of the Kummel. First chill both bottles in the freezer for about one hour. Then, probably as a digestive after a meal, pour a measure of gin carefully into a small wine glass. Follow this with the Kummel – the "Silver Streak" is most attractive as your pour. This drink is usually served without added ice cubes.

GIN GIMLET

☆

1 measure gin
1 measure Rose's lime juice or fresh lime juice
Mint leaves

Chill the gin before use, and place the glasses in the freezer to achieve an attractive "frosted" look. Then carefully pour in the gin, followed by the lime cordial. Stir to blend. If fresh lime juice is used, add a little castor sugar to taste and stir well to dissolve. Garnish with fresh mint leaves.

HAWAIIAN

☆ ☆

2 measures gin
½ measure orange juice
½ measure pineapple juice
½ measure orange curaçao
*   liqueur*
Soda water (optional)
Orange slices and pineapple
*   pieces (garnish)*

Place ice cubes in the shaker and shake all ingredients together, except for the soda water. Strain into a short tumbler and add soda if a fizzy cocktail is preferred. Any traditional orange liqueur may be used in this recipe. Garnish with various fruit slices.

FALLEN ANGEL

☆ ☆

2 measures gin
Juice of 1 lemon
2 dashes green crème de menthe
*   liqueur*
1 dash Angostura Bitters

This is a typical 1920s style "daring" concoction in its use of sweet crème de menthe, but balanced with the bitters it is very drinkable. Place ice cubes in shaker and shake all ingredients well – then strain into a cocktail glass. Decorate with an olive if desired.

65

MONKEY GLAND

☆ ☆

2 measures gin
1 measure orange juice
3 dashes Pernod or similar anise
    drink
3 dashes grenadine non-
    alcoholic fruit cordial

The name of this cocktail dates it
to the 1920s and it had quite a
reputation as an aphrodisiac –
hence the title "monkey gland,"
as these glands were supposed
to give you eternal youth and
vigour. To try this potion yourself,
pour ingredients in order listed
over ice in your shaker, then
shake well and strain into a fairly
large cocktail glass or an old-
fashioned champagne "coupe."
No garnish is necessary.

BRONX

☐ OR ☐ ☐ ☆ ☆

1 measure gin
½ measure dry vermouth
½ measure sweet vermouth
Juice of ½ orange
Dash of grenadine (if required)
(Optional) soda water
Orange slice and cocktail cherry
    (garnish)

This drink is also known as "The
Perfect Martini" but it is only
perfect for those with a sweet
tooth. The grenadine adds extra
red colour and sweetness so you
can decide whether it is to your
own taste by experiment. Place
ice cubes in a shaker then add
gin, the two styles of vermouth
and the orange juice, and shake
well. Strain into a cocktail glass
for a short drink or a tumbler for a
longer drink. Add grenadine and
soda to taste. Garnish with
orange slices and cocktail cherry.

SINGAPORE GIN SLING

OR

2 measures gin
1 measure cherry brandy
1½ measures lemon juice
1 teaspoon castor sugar
Soda water to taste
Cherry and straws to garnish
   (plus umbrellas and other
   fantasies)

This eminently drinkable mix may
be too much for your guests on a
hot day, or before lunch, so do
feel free to reduce the gin
measure to one; but be sure to
reduce the lemon juice to one
measure, and the cherry brandy
to ½ measure. Place ice cubes in
shaker then add gin, cherry
brandy and lemon juice. Shake
well, then add sugar and shake
rapidly to dissolve. Pour into a tall
tumbler and top up with soda to
taste. Decorate with the full range
of fruit and cocktail accessories
as this is a very pretty drink.

NEGRONI

1 measure gin
1 measure Campari
1 measure sweet vermouth

Pour ingredients in order listed
into a mixing glass and stir gently
with some ice cubes, then strain
into a cocktail glass to serve.
Garnish with a twist of orange
peel.

RUM

The traditional image of rum as a dark, fiery drink for cold winter days is giving way to a new look. White rum has gained in popularity and cocktails made with white rum are promoted by the "jet set." There are many delicious recipes for mixed drinks using rum, including many potent punches which make any party go.

Rum has been associated with the islands of the Caribbean ever since Christopher Columbus first took cuttings of sugar cane there in the late-15th century. Rum is made from molasses, the dark sticky substance which remains after sugar crystals have been extracted from the raw cane. Hence the nickname "cane spirit" and brand names using the word "cane."

Like all early spirits, rum was at first made in a rough-and-ready fashion suited to the tough, swashbuckling sailors who liked to drink it on board ship. One 17th-century diary tells of "rumbullion, alias kill-devil . . . a hot, hellish and terrible liquor." The name "rum" probably came from this slang word meaning riotous behaviour, and the reference to "kill devil" was associated with the natives of the West Indies who used rum as a medicine to ward off evil spirits.

Rum played a vital role as a medicine in the life of U.S. settlers. Without access to qualified doctors they had to rely on home remedies. Rum proved invaluable as an anaesthetic and to dress wounds. Molasses became an important trading commodity. It was shipped from the islands to the mainland for distillation into American rum.

Just before the American Revolution, the British Government levied a heavy tax on molasses and this aggravated attitudes against colonial rule. During the war, American rum-runners regularly breached the British naval blockade to bring in supplies of molasses and rum for the American troops.

The association of rum with the sea continued for a long time in Britain, where all the sailors in the British Navy were issued with a daily "tot" of rum to raise morale. This practice was ended only within the last 20 years. Lime juice was usually added to the rum as a preventative against scurvy (Vitamin C deficiency).

Although no longer an official drink, Naval Rum still exists in Britain, along with many other styles of dark and golden rum. These are shipped as young liquor in wooden casks from the Caribbean, then aged in warehouses until ready. The damp climate is said to lend extra flavour during maturation.

In the United States, rum is still produced on a small scale, including dark rum made from blackstrap molasses in the South. But much of the U.S. rum trade has given way to Caribbean imports, notably of white rum. Sugar cane has never been a major crop here and it is more practical to import a finished rum than the raw molasses, because the sources of supply are not far from the mainland.

The Virgin Islands are used as a "clearing house" for many rums of all three styles: dark, golden and white. Some rum is bottled there then shipped to the United States in cartons, but much is sent in casks for

bottling. This rum often becomes house brands for well-known companies.

Apart from the Caribbean islands, including Jamaica, Haiti, Martinique, and Barbados, rum is also made in South American countries including Guyana and Venezuela.

A GUIDE TO BRANDS

Dark Rums

This is the rum of tradition – "yo-ho-ho and a bottle of rum," sang the pirates in R. L. Stevenson's *Treasure Island*. They meant the dark, warming beverage sold either as Naval Rum or simply dark rum. The quality of these rums may vary widely as may the strength (up to 151 proof).

Look for "Jamaica" on the label if you are seeking a top-quality example of this style. The name on the label means it was genuinely made on the island, and these rums are renowned with rum enthusiasts. The Jamaicans use a special method for preparing their dark rum. They add *dunder*, a dark residue from a previous batch of liquor, to each new batch in the same way as previously fermented yeast and flour were additives for extra flavour in sourdough bread.

This style of rum is excellent in hot punches, but check its strength – anywhere from 86 to 151 proof – and adjust your recipe accordingly. Look for *Myer's* or *Appleton's* Jamaican rum in the United States if you wish to sample the real thing. In Britain, *Lamb's Navy Rum* or *Pusser's* will give you a taste of the sailor's tipple.

The other famous source of dark rum is Guyana, in South America. It is named *Demerara* rum, after the local river, and you may also find golden-coloured sugar crystals with this name. Extra caramel is added to this rum to deepen the colour.

The French have a long history as colonists in the Caribbean islands and they still enjoy a wide range of rums for cooking and drinking. *Rhum Negrita* from Martinique is a favourite in French kitchens as is *Rhum St. James* from the same island. This is sold in the United States at 91 proof in a distinctive square bottle.

You might suppose that the Bacardi family have been millionaires for the past 100 years with such a renowned brand, but in fact their fortunes have been uneven. The company began in 1862 in Cuba. Later the founding family moved to Spain, where they were lucky enough to cure the young heir to the Spanish throne of a fever with their special rum. The company was then granted the right to bear the arms of Spain on their label and this meant fame and fortune for the family and their product. However, their involvement in Cuban politics meant exile when Castro came to power, and the family was forced to move to Puerto Rico.

The transfer to Puerto Rico proved lucky because its proximity to the United States and ease of shipment led to increased sales. From the early 1960s, the phenomenal growth of Bacardi as a brand began in earnest. Additional distilleries were built on Nassau, in the Bahamas, to supply the European market.

Apart from their standard *Carta Blanca* label, Bacardi also market a premium white rum called Añejo (old) which is presented in a special flat-sided flask. They also sell a high-strength white rum at 151 proof for a really heady rum punch. Other Puerto Rican white rums include

Ronrico and *Don Q.*

White rum is also produced to a high-quality standard in Jamaica. Look for the *Appleton* brand. Guyana, Barbados and Trinidad also produce this fashionable style; *Dry Cane* is a blend from these areas. From Martinique comes a French favourite light rum, named "*Old Nick.*" Like the other popular French *rhum*, this is shipped by *Bardinet* of Bordeaux.

Golden rums

These elegant yet full-flavoured rums are readily distinguished on the shelf – they usually have gold-coloured labels.

This is a rum to be savoured straight, or in a simple mixed drink. The best examples come from Jamaica and Cuba (although the latter are not obtainable in the United States). Trinidad and Costa Rica also produce rum and sometimes a bottle will contain a blend of golden rums from various places. This is particularly common in Britain, where casks of several rums have been aged together then blended at the time of bottling.

Basically a golden rum is a light rum which started life as a white rum but was aged in a cask to give it some colour, added aroma and depth of flavour. Well-known labels include *Captain Morgan, Lemon Hart* and two brands best-known for their white rums: *Bacardi* and *Ronrico*.

White rums

Although these rums are colourless, this does not mean that they are ready for sale on the day of production, like vodka or gin. Many are aged in wood casks. They differ from golden or dark rum in that these casks are not charred so the colour transfers very gradually, so little as to be imperceptible.

These more delicate rums are high fashion today, but they are not new. They have a shorter history than traditional rum, certainly, but can still trace their origins back some 100 years. The name of *Bacardi* has become a universally-known title for white rum in general. People order a "Bacardi and Coke," rather than a "white rum with cola." Such is the power of marketing and familiarity of a certain brand.

HOW TO SERVE RUM

Although rum has been served in mixed drinks almost since its invention, there are still occasions when a glass of really good rum may be offered in the same way as a fine French cognac or Scotch single malt whisky. Serve in a small balloon glass and warm with your hands while sipping slowly. This is a pleasant drink for a winter evening, perhaps after a day in the open air.

SAILOR'S GROG

☐ OR 🍵   ☆

1 measure dark rum
2 measures cold water
Juice of 1 lemon
½ teaspoon sugar
Strip of orange rind
4 cloves
Cinnamon stick

Put all ingredients in a pan and
heat gently. Do not allow to boil.
Serve with a cinnamon stick as
stirrer. Traditionally this drink
would have been served in a
pewter tankard and heated by
plunging a red-hot iron poker into
the drink. Guaranteed to
raise the
temperature!

RUM TODDY

☐ OR 🍵🥄   ☆

1 measure dark rum
1 cup hot tea
3 cloves

Stir all ingredients together, then
strain and serve in a pewter
tankard or glass mug. For **Hot
Buttered Rum** add a
½ teaspoon of butter and stir in
well.

BALTIMORE EGG NOG

1 measure dark rum
1 egg
1½ teaspoons sugar
½ measure Madeira wine
1 cup fresh milk
Dash of grated nutmeg

Warm milk, then stir in rum, followed by egg and sugar. Add Madeira. Pour into tall tumbler and sprinkle on nutmeg. For extra effect, whisk with small hand whisk before adding nutmeg. This drink is traditional at Christmas time and incorporates the two favourite drinks of the American Founding Fathers – Rum and Madeira. It may also be made with brandy. In summer, try an ice-cold version, by shaking all ingredients together with ice, then pouring into a tall tumbler. Try ground cinnamon as an alternative garnish.

DAIQUIRI

2 measures white rum
Juice of ½ lime or ¼ lemon
1 teaspoon castor sugar
(Optional) egg white

Place some ice cubes in a blender goblet, then add other ingredients. Blend until all ice is crushed and other ingredients well-mixed. Pour into a short tumbler.

PIÑA COLADA

2 measures white rum (may also
  be made with dark rum)
3 tablespoons crushed pineapple
3 tablespoons coconut milk
Dash Angostura bitters
Pineapple pieces, lime slices to
  garnish

Note: If coconut milk is difficult to
obtain, use cream of coconut and
mix with water first to obtain a
liquid.

Pour the rum over cracked ice
into your blender goblet, then
add the pineapple and coconut.
Blend until well-mixed. Pour into
a tall tumbler and serve with a
straw and plenty of decoration,
including pineapple pieces, lime
slices and perhaps a paper
umbrella. Alternatively, should
you have a whole pineapple
available, hollow it out and use to
serve this special drink.

BACARDI COCKTAIL

1 measure white rum
½ measure lime juice
½ measure grenadine
Cocktail cherry (garnish)

Place ice cubes in shaker, then
add all ingredients. Shake well
and strain into a cocktail glass.

PLANTER'S PUNCH

 ☆ ☆

2 measures light or dark rum
½ measure grenadine
1 measure lime juice
1 measure orange juice
Soda water (optional)

Fill a tall tumbler with crushed ice, then pour in all ingredients. Stir well, then add soda water to taste. A traditional planter's punch would be made with dark rum and without the soda water. Garnish with cocktail cherries and orange slices.

PETITE FLEUR

 ☆ ☆

1 measure white rum
1 measure Cointreau or Triple Sec (orange liqueur)
1 measure grapefruit juice
Twist of orange peel (garnish)

White rum is the perfect partner to all fruit flavours. This recipe balances sweet and sharp tastes very well. Place some ice cubes in your shaker, then pour in all ingredients and shake well. Strain into a cocktail glass.

MAI TAI

 ☆ ☆ ☆

1 measure white rum
½ measure dark rum
½ measure tequila
½ measure Triple Sec
1 jigger apricot brandy (liqueur)
1 measure orange juice
1 dash Angostura bitters
2 dashes grenadine

Here is a really complicated drink which tastes deceptively simple and innocuous. Guests coming back for a second should be warned! To prepare, pour all ingredients but the bitters into a blender goblet with cracked ice. Blend until smooth. Pour into a tall tumbler and garnish liberally with orange slices, cocktail cherries and cocktail accessories.

SANTA CRUZ FIX

 ☆ ☆

1 measure dark rum
½ measure cherry brandy
  (liqueur)
1 teaspoon castor sugar
1 teaspoon water
Juice of ½ lemon

Stir together the water and sugar in a tall tumbler until dissolved. Fill the tumbler with crushed ice, then pour in all remaining ingredients. Stir with a swizzle stick. Serve with a straw.

ZOMBIE

 ☆ ☆ ☆

1 measure white rum
1 measure dark rum
1 measure apricot brandy
(liqueur)
½ measure orange juice
½ measure lemon juice
½ measure pineapple juice

The name of this drink reveals its origin, on the island of Haiti, where natives still believe the myths of the "living dead." As with the Mai Tai, the smooth flavour of this blend belies its strength. Pour all ingredients over cracked ice in a blender goblet, then blend until well-mixed. Serve in a tall tumbler, or in a hollowed-out pineapple.

CUBA LIBRA

☆

1 measure white rum
1 tablespoon unsweetened lime
juice
Cola

Pour over ice in tall glass, top with cola and add a twist of lime or lemon rind.

BRANDY

Here is a spirit which is often favoured by wine drinkers. After all,
brandy is the essence of wine after it has been reduced by distillation.
Brandy is an ancient spirit produced in a simplified form in Greece and
Rome before the birth of Christ, but it was not used as a beverage until
the Middle Ages. The greatest brandies of the world are made in
France, including cognac and armagnac, top-quality fine spirits for the
connoisseur.

Sometimes the term "brandy" can be a little confusing. Apart from
a straightforward grape brandy, made with wine, there are also other
fruit brandies, such as apricot or cherry. Strictly speaking, these are
not true brandies, but cordials with added sweeteners and flavouring
(see page 94 for more details).

The word "brandy" is derived from a Dutch term meaning "burnt
wine" and one reason why brandy proved successful during the
Renaissance period of the 15th and 16th centuries was ease of
shipment. At that time wine almost always turned sour during a sea
voyage, so that distilled spirit such as brandy became preferred. In
addition, it was discovered that the wood casks used for shipment
actually improved the spirit and added smooth qualities to its taste.
This principle is used to this day to mature fine brandy and other spirits
such as whiskies.

FRENCH BRANDIES

All styles of brandy are made in France. These vary in price and quality
from the finest liqueur brandies to inexpensive grape brandies for
mixed drinks and cooking. Although the top brandies are called
"liqueur," this does not mean they are sweetened or flavoured. They
are simply the best available and meant to be drunk straight. When
selecting a French brandy for home use, bear in mind your preference
in drinks. It is a waste to mix superior cognac into a cocktail. On the
other hand, simple grape brandy is disappointing served after a meal in
a balloon glass.

COGNAC

This special brandy has been made in the region around the town of
Cognac, in western France, since the 17th century. Before that time,
dry white wine was made there, but it was found to spoil during
shipment, so distillation was tried as a way of preserving the wine. The
result was a far better drink, which became very popular in Britain. It
was sold everywhere in London, often from stalls in the street. Drinkers
of that period mixed their brandy with water, and it was often served
warm. The Scandinavians also developed a passion for cognac, and
eventually exports to North America began.

Within the region there are specially defined sub-regions which
grow grapes destined to become cognac. These include "Grande
Champagne" and "Petite Champagne", meaning large and small

meadow, which is why cognac labels often mention "Champagne." This simply means that the bottle contains brandy made in these two top-quality zones of production. There is no connection with Champagne wine, which is made in northern France around the town of Reims.

Cognac is always blended using elements from many casks to develop a particular flavour associated with a certain "marque" or brand. Whatever the quality of the bottle of cognac you select, it is always a blend – there are no "straight" cognacs, as there would be straight whiskies. Similarly, there are no vintage dates as you would see on a bottle of wine, for elements are taken from casks of different ages to give the desired taste.

As a general rule, the more expensive "liqueur" brandies contain a higher proportion of old brandy. Old brandies are stored in barrels for many decades, and a visit to a cognac distillery is well worthwhile to see (and breathe in) the amazing rows of these ancient casks, all made of local oak.

HOW TO READ A COGNAC LABEL

Labels on cognac bottles can be confusing, and it is hard to establish which level of quality you are looking at. There are two helpful indicators; the "star" system and initials such as V.S.O.P.

Basic cognac sold outside France will probably be a **three-star** quality, meaning it has spent at least three years aging in a wood cask. In addition, it will bear initials confirming the age, usually **V.S.**, meaning Very Special.

Finer cognacs will bear the initials **V.S.O.P.** and possibly four or five stars. There is no hard and fast rule about these initials and star markings, so let price be your guide when it comes to comparisons. And try to learn the names of some reliable shippers of a style of cognac you find enjoyable. Incidentally, V.S.O.P means Very Superior Old Pale.

Some well-known cognac houses include *Martell*, established in 1715, with a V.S.O.P. cognac called "Medaillon"; *Courvoisier*, promoted as "the brandy of Napoleon"; *Hennessy*, founded by an Irishman in 1765; *Remy Martin*, a marketing triumph of the past ten years, although it is also a very old house; and *Bisquit* and *Hine*, paler cognacs for those who prefer a lighter taste.

Some confusion surrounds the use of the name **Napoleon** on cognac bottles. "Napoleon brandy" has no legal meaning, and is not an indication of special quality. However, many firms do offer a deluxe blend with a high proportion of old brandies and these may bear the title "Napoleon." To be sure, look for some initials as well: **V.O.** means Very Old; **X.O.** or **X.X.O.** are Extra Old. This last category will include cognac of great age, 50 years or more, with a price to match. It would make a lovely gift for a true cognac enthusiast, but at home a V.S.O.P. normally represents the best value for drinking straight after meals.

ARMAGNAC

This is famous as the brandy preferred by the Three Musketeers, and it has been made in Gascony for even longer than cognac. Experts generally contrast them by describing armagnac as "earthy" and pungent, while cognac is slightly lighter in flavour and more stylish. Armagnac tastes more fruity than cognac, with a scent of ripe plums.

Of course, it is made only from grapes grown in particular areas established over the centuries. The Moors of North Africa made their way to this corner of south-west France in the Middle Ages and passed on their secrets of distillation. Until the early 20th century, the brandy of this region was often sent north for blending with cognac, but now strict regulations govern production of both styles, and the two distinct tastes are recognized worldwide.

HOW TO READ AN ARMAGNAC LABEL

Like cognac, armagnac is aged in local oak casks after distillation. But unlike many other spirits, including cognac, it is distilled only once in traditional pot stills used only in this area, so a good deal of the base flavour of the wine remains in the spirit.

The titles used on labels are similar to those used for cognac, with **three-star** the usual style; **V.S.O.P.** the next in quality; and then other top quality bottlings with **Extra** or **Hors d'Age** on the label. Like cognac, nearly all armagnac is blended from the various sub-regions (*Bas Armagnac, Haut Armagnac* and *Tenareze*), and bears no vintage date.

The style of bottle used differs too; most armagnac is sold in flat-sided flasks with a long neck, while cognac has a more rounded bottle with square "shoulders."

Many armagnac bottles are "frosted" by a special blasting process to give an attractive appearance and some have unusual twisted necks and wax seals which make them good gifts for a "friend who has everything."

OTHER FRENCH BRANDIES

Many people believe that a drop of brandy is good for you, and certainly brandy does appear to calm the nerves after a sudden crisis. In Europe, it is common practice to keep a bottle of brandy in the kitchen for "medicinal purposes," and for cooking. It is amazing how much better a simple casserole of beef can taste when a spoonful of brandy is added and flamed before placing it in the oven; and brandy has no parallel as an agent for flambé dishes served at the table. In Britain, brandy is poured over the Christmas pudding and then set alight as it is carried into a darkened room, to spectacular effect.

For all these purposes, a simple **grape brandy** is quite adequate, or a three-star cognac or armagnac for elegant dinner-party flambés. You will find that grape brandies made in other parts of France will be quite suitable in the kitchen, and for mixed drinks with several added ingredients.

Apart from grape brandy, another style of brandy made in France (and in Italy and Germany) is **marc**. This is made with the dregs remaining after wine has fermented. It has a full and noticeable aroma which has been called "barnyard" by those who do not like it, and "delicious" by those who do. It is named after the region of production. For instance, a marc made from Burgundy wine dregs (pomace) is called *Marc de Bourgogne*; one from Champagne is *Marc* *de Champagne*; and in Alsace it is *Marc de Gewutztraminer*, named for the grape variety.

GUIDE TO BRANDS

For armagnac, look for well-known houses including *Janneau, Marquis de Montesoiou, Malliac* and *Sempé*.

For grape brandy, look for a bottle called *"Fine,"* priced lower than cognac or armagnac. In Britain, *Three Barrels* is well known.

BRANDIES OF EUROPE

Among other European countries, notable brandy producers include Italy, where **grappa** is their popular version of marc; Spain, where this is a favoured spirit, often confusingly labelled **conac**; and Germany, where local brandies are made with wines made in neighbouring countries, bought in at low rates. Brandy is also made in Greece, where *Metaxa* is the leading brand name. The German brandy most widely distributed abroad is *Asbach Uralt*, and Spanish *Fundador* is also sold worldwide.

AMERICAN BRANDY

More brandy is made in the United States than in France, most of it in California. A good deal of California brandy is of fairly modest quality, but some have enough depth of flavour to rival fine cognac and armagnac. In general, California brandy has a slightly sweeter taste than European equivalents.

The first brandies made in California were produced by early missionaries from native grapes, but once wine-making improved, so did the quality of the brandy. Wines made in the hot climate of California's Central Valley are distilled because they have too "oily" a taste for table wine. Today three out of four bottles of brandy bought in the United States are American.

Leading Brands include *The Christian Brothers*, a genuine religious organization that also makes excellent wine. This is the best-selling brandy in the United States. Other wine companies who produce good brandy include *Paul Masson; Almaden;* and *California Wine Association*, with their *A.R. Morrow* and *Aristocrat* brands.

Other favourite labels include *Lejon*, a premium bottling, *De Kuyper,* and *E.M.J.,* a less expensive brand, as well as a host of house labels, all light styles suitable for use in mixed drinks.

BRANDY AROUND THE WORLD

Wherever wine is made, local brandies are also available. In South Africa brandy is the national favourite for spirit drinkers. A sweet, heavy style is preferred, and well-known brands include *Paarl Five Star, Castle,* and *Bertrams*. A large South African wine-making organization, *K.W.V.*, is also a major brandy distiller, and offers a range of styles from three-star to 10-year-old.

Australian wine is also used as a base for distillation into brandy. At first, brandy was only made when too much wine had been produced, but today brandy has a place on the home market, and a little is sent abroad. Like South Africans, Australians like their brandy on the sweet side. Brands include *Great Western, St. Agnes, Remy* and *Hennesssy*; the last two are made in association with the French companies who produce cognac.

In South America, Peru is noted for its *pisco* brandy, which is a colourless spirit made from pomace, like French *marc*. It is sold in a distinctive bottle shaped like an Inca carving. Mexican brandy is made in great quantities, and to variable quality standards, but the best are light and pleasant in cocktails. *Presidente* is the leading brand.

HOW TO SERVE BRANDIES

Top-quality cognac and armagnac should always be served straight, without water or ice. Unlike gin and vodka, which are at their best when cold, or whiskey, which may be offered chilled or at room temperature, fine brandy is actually best when quite warm. The ideal temperature is body heat, so warm the brandy glass in your hands as you revolve it slowly in your palm.

A complex ritual has arisen around the serving of fine cognac and armagnac, as well as the best California brandies. In elegant restaurants of Europe and America you will notice these expensive spirits being served in giant "balloon" glasses, and sometimes being warmed over a flame at the table. All of this does create an atmosphere of glamour and romance, but in truth is not really ideal for the actual taste of the brandy.

At home, use a small balloon glass or a "tulip" shape wine glass as a brandy snifter. Choose the thinnest glass or crystal you can afford so that the heat from your hand will transfer readily to the brandy. Applying extra heat from a spirit lamp is not advisable because you could lose a good deal of your priceless glassful by evaporation!

BRANDY IN THE KITCHEN

Brandy is an indispensable part of any kitchen cupboard. You can use it for making all types of flambé dishes, from Steak Diane to Crepes Suzette, and for marinading meat for casseroles. In addition, it is an ideal spirit to use for preserving fruits. Any freshly-picked fruit (plums and peaches are ideal) may be left to marinade in inexpensive brandy with a little sugar and the result is a delectable dessert, after a month or so. Note: with the really low-priced brandies you need add very little sugar. They are already sweetened.

BETWEEN THE SHEETS

1 measure brandy
1 measure white or golden rum
1 measure Cointreau or Triple
    Sec (orange liqueur)
Dash of lemon juice
Cocktail cherry and lemon slice
    (garnish)

Shake all ingredients together
with ice cubes in the shaker.
Strain into a chilled cocktail glass.
Garnish with cocktail cherry and
lemon slice. This is a typical
recipe from the classic age of
cocktails in the 1920s and should
be sampled with caution by the
inexperienced cocktail drinker!

BRONX

1 measure brandy (use California
    brandy if available)
½ measure sweet vermouth
½ measure dry vermouth
Cocktail cherry (garnish)

Place ice cubes in shaker, then
add brandy and vermouths.
Shake well and strain into a
chilled cocktail glass. Decorate
with a cherry and paper umbrella
if available. Note: This drink may
also be made with gin, or mix a
half measure of brandy with a half
measure of gin for a lighter, drier
version.

SIDE CAR

 ☆ ☆

1 measure brandy
½ measure Cointreau or Triple
  Sec (orange liqueur)
½ measure lemon juice
Dash of sugar syrup or castor
  sugar (optional)

Place ice cubes in shaker then
shake all ingredients together.
Strain into a chilled cocktail glass.
If more sweetness is required,
add a dash of sugar syrup or stir
in castor sugar until thoroughly
dissolved. Garnish with lemon
peel if desired.

BRANDY ALEXANDER

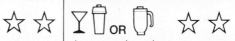 ☆ ☆

1 measure brandy
1 measure crème de cacao or Tia
  Maria (liqueur)
1 measure thick cream (or
  whipping cream)
Grated nutmeg (optional) or
  powdered cinnamon (garnish)

Here is one of the irresistible and
calorific cocktails made with thick
cream, which make a perfect end
to a dinner party. Make sure the
cream you use is very fresh and
always serve this drink
immediately after mixing to avoid
ingredients separating. Place a
few ice cubes in your shaker, then
pour in other ingredients in the
order given above. Shake well
and strain into a cocktail glass.
For a more frothy effect, use
whipping cream and make the
cocktail in your blender. When
serving, sprinkle a little nutmeg
on the finished drink (or
powdered cinnamon if preferred).

85

BLUE ANGEL

1 measure brandy
½ measure blue curacao
   (liqueur)
½ measure Parfait Amour
   (liqueur)
Dash lemon juice
1 measure thick cream

Place ice cubes in shaker and
add all ingredients, then shake
well and serve at once in a large
cocktail glass. This drink is a
glorious creamy blue and very
refreshing.

FOXHOUND

1 measure brandy
½ measure cranberry juice
¼ measure Kummel (caraway
   liqueur)
Dash lemon juice
Lemon slice (garnish)

This cocktail is traditionally
served after a hard day's hunting,
before sampling the day's catch
at dinner. Place ice cubes in
shaker, then pour in all
ingredients and shake well; strain
and serve in a wine glass.

HORSE'S NECK

1 measure brandy
Dash of Angostura bitters
Ginger ale to taste
Spiral of lemon peel

Another refreshing recipe
connected with outdoor sport.
Hang a continuous spiral of
lemon peel in a tall tumbler. Add
ice and then brandy. Add a dash
of bitters and stir, then top with
ginger ale to taste. *Note:* This
may also be made with whisky,
gin or light rum.

PICK ME UP

1 measure brandy
1 whole egg
½ measure curaçao (orange
  liqueur)
2 measures fresh milk

Shake the brandy, egg and
curaçao together, then strain into
a short tumbler. Add the milk and
stir. Serve with a straw. *Note:* This
mixture is excellent for loss of
appetite and in convalescence. It
also makes a delicious brunch
drink.

TEQUILA &

Tequila

Here is a case of a cocktail inventing the spirit. Tequila was virtually unknown outide Central America until a fashion for the Margarita, and later, the Tequila Sunrise, caught on during the 1970s. Since then it has increased its sales and is now a major spirit in both Britain and the United States.

In reality, tequila is an ancient drink, first made by the Aztecs of Mexico, then by their Spanish conquerors. It is produced from the heart of the *agave*, a giant succulent plant which grows in near-desert conditions around the Mexican town of Tequila. Like French cognac, this spirit must come from a strictly-defined area to bear the authentic title Tequila.

There are two tequila styles: white and gold. The white is sold soon after production and has light flavour with the typically spicy aroma of this spirit. Gold tequila is aged in wood vats for at least nine months, and some caramel is then added to improve the colour. The finest tequila is called *anejo*, meaning old; drink this straight, like brandy.

There are two major brands of tequila: *Josè Cuervo* and *Sauza*. They market both styles of tequila worldwide. But now American liquor firms are entering this growing market, with companies such as Jim Beam selling *Beamero Tequila*. There are also house brands.

HOW TO SERVE TEQUILA

The classic Mexican way of drinking tequila involves a good deal of practice. First chill a bottle of tequila and some small glasses.

Then pour a measure of tequila (white or gold) into the glass. Cut a lime in half and hold it in your left hand. Then sprinkle a little salt onto your left hand in the space between your thumb and forefinger. Hold the glass of tequila in your right hand. Lick the salt off your hand, then toss back the tequila and quickly suck the lime. Once you practise, you can try accomplishing this with one hand! The trick is to do all three actions as rapidly as possible.

A development of this idea is the **Margarita** cocktail (see page 91).

OTHER FRUIT SPIRITS

An extraordinary variety of spirits are made the world over from all manner of fruits and even vegetables. People have found ways of converting almost any crop into a pleasant drink, and although some may be hard to find, it is fascinating to try them all, perhaps when travelling.

For instance, in Mexico, tequila is not the only native spirit. Mezcal is another, made from an agave-heart wine called *pulque*. It is extremely powerful and has a resemblance to brandy. It is traditionally bottled with a worm in the base of the bottle. This worm is said to give great power to anyone with sufficient courage to gulp it down.

In Hawaii, there is *Okolehao*, made from the

root of the sacred Ti plant. It is now made with modern methods and often enjoyed by tourists on the islands, who regularly mix it with Coca-Cola, to make an *Oke & Coke*.

Even more ancient than these is rice brandy, made in China and Japan. In China it is distilled from fermented rice to make a powerful spirit, served slightly warm. Japanese *sake* is also served warm, but is not strictly speaking a spirit because it has not been distilled.

But fruits are more widely used as the basis for these fiery yet fragrant spirits. It is important to know what you are buying. Some bottles labelled "Apricot Brandy" for instance, are liqueurs, with added flavourings and sweeteners. So consult this list before you buy.

APPLE

Applejack is a well-known drink in North America and Europe. In France, **Calvados** is made in a strictly limited area and with tight quality control exactly like cognac or armagnac, except it is made with apples, not grapes. The region with the best examples is the Pays d'Auge in Normandy. This warming drink is commonly served after a meal at room temperature, but may also be mixed with soda and poured over ice if desired. It also makes a marvellous aid in the kitchen, particularly when cooking pork dishes. The apple taste and tartness cuts the richness of the meat. Look for *Père Magloire, Boulard,* and *Arc de Triomphe* brands, but it is best to buy a medium-priced bottle rather than the cheapest. The basic Calvados can be too pungent.

In America, it is New England and especially Canada which have perfected the art of making **applejack**. Long ago, it was made by freezing apple cider (the alcoholic type), until it was concentrated into a raw spirit. Freezing is an alternative to the heat, usually applied during distillation, but of course it is far from ideal as the quality of the spirit cannot be monitored. Today applejack is blended with at least 50 per cent neutral grain alcohol to give a lighter taste than the French traditional style. Serve it over ice. Look for *Laird* and *Spea* brands.

CHERRY

Here is a confusing bottle: if it is labelled Cherry Brandy it will be a liqueur (often dark red due to added artificial colouring), but a clear spirit labelled cherry or **Kirsch** is a dry drink. True Kirsch is a drink of exceptional quality, made in Germany, the Alsace region of France, and in Switzerland. Kirsch is often used in cooking and, if this is the use you have in mind, look for *Kirsch Fantaisie*, which is simply pure spirit with cherry flavouring. It marries well with fresh pineapple. But to sample the classic European style, you will need to pay more and buy a reputable brand such as *Bols* or *Dettling*. Serve it ice cold in tiny glasses as you would *Schnapps* or imported vodka.

OTHER WHITE FRUIT SPIRITS

In France, these are known as *alcools*, mainly produced in the Alsace region from an extraordinary variety of fruits, including plums, pears and raspberries. Try them all when you visit France, but meanwhile expect to find a limited selection in your own area. **Poire William** is fairly widely sold, and well worth savouring as an occasional after-dinner drink. Serve well-chilled and keep the opened bottle in the refrigerator to preserve its freshness. *Kammer*, a German brand, is often exported.

Plum liquor is also made in Yugoslavia from rather special plums, then aged in wood casks before bottling. It is called **slivovitz**.

TEQUILA SUNRISE

2 measures white or gold tequila
4 measures orange juice
½ measure grenadine syrup
Orange slice (garnish)

Fill a tall tumbler with ice cubes or crushed ice, then pour in tequila and orange juice. Stir well and allow to settle, then gently add grenadine. It will swirl to make an attractive pattern: the "sunrise." As its name suggests, this makes a delightful brunch drink. Garnish with an orange slice.

MARGARITA

1 ½ measures white tequila
½ measure Cointreau or Triple Sec orange liqueur
1 measure lime juice, freshly-squeezed if possible

Chill the cocktail glass in advance, then moisten the rim and dip into fine sea salt to make a frosted edge to the glass (see page 89). Place ice cubes in shaker then add other ingredients. Shake well and strain carefully into glass. Serve immediately as the frosted rim will not last long!

CORCOVADO

☆ ☆ ☆

1 measure white tequila
1 measure blue curacao
1 measure Drambuie whisky
   liqueur
Lemon/lime soda or sparkling
   mineral water
Lime slice (garnish)

Place ice cubes in shaker then
add all ingredient but soda.
Shake well and strain into a tall
tumbler. Add soda to taste, or
mineral water if a less sweet taste
is preferred. Garnish with a lime
slice and perhaps a blue
umbrella. The colour of this drink
is truly eye-catching and it would
be marvellous served by a
swimming pool on a hot day.

VIVA MARIA

☆

1 measure tequila
¼ measure Maraschino (white
   cherry liqueur)
½ measure lime juice
½ teaspoon grenadine syrup
½ egg white

Put all ingredients into the
blender goblet with some
cracked ice, then blend until
smooth. Strain into a large
cocktail glass or wine goblet. This
drink is the most delicate shade
of rose pink with a foaming effect
from the egg white. No added
decoration is needed.

NORMANDY

☆ ☆

1 measure Calvados
½ measure Cointreau or Triple
Sec (orange liqueur)
1 dash grenadine
1 dash lemon juice
1 measure thick cream (chilled)

Place ice cubes in shaker, then
add all ingredients and shake
well. Strain into a cocktail glass
and serve at once. Garnish with
orange slice if desired. A
marvellous substitute for dessert!

BURLINGTON

☆ ☆ ☆

1 measure Calvados
1 measure sweet vermouth
2 measures dry red wine
Soda water
Orange slice (garnish)

Place ice cubes in a tall glass then
pour in Calvados, vermouth and
wine. Stir gently and add soda as
desired. Decorate with a slice of
orange and add
a straw.

LIQUEURS

These rather special sweet drinks have a long history. In medieval times, monks made sweetened concoctions with added herbs and spices as medicines, used in the treatment of complaints as serious as the Plague and as everyday as a broken heart! Liqueurs were also used to flavour foods, especially custards and puddings. Those made with certain ingredients such as mint and caraway were meant as digestives, to be sipped slowly after a rich meal.

Liqueurs, Cordials and Digestifs
There is sometimes confusion in the mind of the consumer when choosing a liqueur. Is a cordial the same type of drink? In the United States the answer is yes. A cordial is merely another word for liqueur, meaning a spirit with added flavourings and sweetenings. Under American law, it must contain at least 2½ per cent sugar to be classified as such. But in Britain, a cordial may be a non-alcoholic drink such as Rose's Lime Juice, which is a fruit syrup. In France, a liqueur may also be described as a *digestif*, a reference to its continued use today as an after-dinner stomach soother.

STYLES OF LIQUEURS AND CORDIALS
As will be seen in the following pages, liqueurs and cordials are of varying styles. All they have in common is a degree of strength (which may vary from 25 to 45 GL proof (U.S. 50 to 90)), a certain sweetness and a richness of flavour. But they may be made from any spirit, or simply a plain base spirit with no flavour of its own. Flavourings added may range from peppermint to apricot to honey and even tea and coffee. Modern inventions include the delicious cream liqueurs such as *Bailey's Irish Cream*, now a world bestseller and rivalling established favourites such as *Benedictine*, which has a long history dating back to the early 16th century.

Brands to look for include well-known European names such as *Bols, Cusenier, De Kuyper* and *Marie Brizard*. In the United States, cordials are marketed under such brand names as *Hiram Walker, Leroux, Dumont* and *Dubouchette*. All these companies offer each style of liqueur, including favourites such as *Crème de Menthe* and *Apricot Brandy*, with less well-known types such as nut liqueurs and perhaps even a banana liqueur. Some of these are especially intended for use in cooking.

Apart from these large companies with an entire portfolio of styles, there are the famous names which stand alone: these include *Drambuie, Southern Comfort, Cointreau* and *Grand Marnier*. These brand leaders are much imitated but rarely rivalled in sales. But when it comes to using liqueurs in mixed drinks, look for a less expensive brand, perhaps under a house label.

THE RANGE OF FLAVOURS
Chocolate, Coffee and Cream
Because these flavours are irresistible to those with a "sweet tooth,"

Mocha Flip ingredients

this category includes some of the top favourites today. It is a good idea to keep at least one bottle from this section on hand for mixing and for offering to anyone who likes a rich after-dinner drink.

Coffee liqueurs have an intense flavour and are usually highly sweetened. They are wonderful when served over ice cream or added to black coffee. European coffee liqueurs are called *crème de cafe, mokka* or perhaps *crème de mocha*, and all the top liqueur companies sell their own version. There is even a *Mokka mit Sahne* (Coffee and Cream) a deliciously rich German cordial which combines coffee and real cream. But in the United States, as elsewhere, *Kahlua* is the major name for coffee liqueurs. Made in Mexico (or in Europe under license by the Peter Heering company of Denmark), it is rich and heavy with a pungent taste of true Mexican coffee. The other famous coffee liqueur, a bestseller in Britain, is *Tia Maria*, made in Jamaica and slightly lighter than Kahlua. *Jameson's Irish Velvet* is an interesting mixture, including coffee liqueur with Jameson's Irish whiskey. Try it in a cup of fresh coffee with double cream for an extra rich Irish Coffee.

Chocolate liqueurs have been popular since the days of the Aztec kings and of course were once for the rich only. Now we can all sample *Crème de Cacao*, as it is called in Europe. It may be colourless or have added colouring to turn it a chocolate brown. In the United States *Hiram Walker* and *Leroux* have a full range of chocolate liqueurs with extra flavourings such as cherry, banana and mint. And the house of *Hallgarten* sells a delicious range of *Royal Chocolate* liqueurs with added flavour; *Royal Mint Chocolate* is the best known, but *Royal Orange Chocolate* and even *Royal Nut Chocolate* are a different taste experience. Other well-known chocolate flavoured liqueurs include *Sabra* from Israel and *Vandermint*, which mixes mint flavour with chocolate, sold in an attractive Delft-style stoneware flask.

Cream liqueurs have been a success story of the past decade. They are irresistible after-dinner drinks, or they may be used in cocktails and served over ice as a long drink.

Cream is also an ingredient of some high-calorie mixed drinks like the **Grasshopper** and the **Alexander**, so I have included a few recipes for these with this section. The reason a pre-mixed cream liqueur was not sold until comparatively recently is that it was difficult to keep a mixture of spirit and cream stable in the bottle. Once this technical hitch was overcome, delicious mixes such as Irish whiskey and fresh cream (the principal ingredients of *Bailey's Irish Cream*) were possible. *Bailey's* is now a top seller worldwide, with *American Cream*, an American rival made by Heublein, and *Carolan's*, an Irish competitor. Another Irish product is *Royal Tara Irish Cream* which incorporates a hint of orange with the other ingredients; and then there is *Waterford Cream*, which its noticeable whiskey flavour.

Cream liqueurs are not always made with whiskey; brandy is another base. *Greensleeves* is made in London from a subtle blend of French brandy, Devon cream and mint. It is a pale green in colour. A richer taste is *Chantre*, made in Germany from brandy and cream.

For those who have never tried any of these new liqueurs, consider Jim Beam's *Gaetano Creme Liqueur*, a low-priced mixture of whiskey and cream.

Before cream could be successfully mixed with spirit, a similar texture was obtained in liqueurs by using eggs. Drinks with egg have always been viewed as "health drinks," and they are certainly ideal to offer to anyone who has suffered loss of appetite. The Dutch excel at making these mixtures of egg and spirit, called *Advocaat*. All the Dutch liqueurs houses such as *Bols* make one. This drink is also made in Spain and Mexico – where it is called *Rompope*. Try mixing it with fresh or canned fruit to make an unusual fruit salad.

Coconut liqueurs have also caught on in the past ten years. They are smooth white drinks with a creamy consistency, but do not actually contain cream. Examples are *Malibu* and *Cocoribe*. Their rum base makes them an ideal agent for mixing rich and exotic cocktails. Coconut may also be mixed with chocolate as in *Chococo* from the Virgin Islands.

MOCHA FLIP

2 measures Kahlua or Tia Maria
1 egg yolk
1 tablespoon cream
½ cup shaved ice
Grated nutmeg (garnish)

Place all ingredients except nutmeg in the blender and mix thoroughly for 20 seconds. Serve in a goblet with a sprinkle of nutmeg for a lovely brunch drink or alternative to dessert.

KAHLUA KISS

☆ ☆

1 ½ measures Kahlua
1 dash crème de noyaux nut
 liqueur
Thick cream

Fill the cocktail glass with
crushed ice, then pour in the
Kahlua. Add the crème de
noyaux and then float a good
dash of thick cream on top. Do
not stir as this will spoil the
appearance of the drink. *Note:* Be
sure the cream is absolutely
fresh.

GRASSHOPPER

☆ ☆

1 measure white crème de cacao
1 measure green crème de
 menthe
1 measure cream
Shaved chocolate (garnish)

Place ice cubes in shaker, then all
ingredients in order listed. Shake
well and strain into a cocktail
glass. Sprinkle shaved chocolate
onto surface of this attractively
tinted drink. Truly refreshing
despite the richness of the
cream.

ACAPULCO

☆ ☆ ☆

1 measure Kahlua or Tia Maria
1 measure tequila
1 measure Cocoribe or Malibu
  coconut liqueur

Place ice cubes in shaker, then add all ingredients and shake well. Strain into a short tumbler over crushed ice. This is a rich combination which really makes your worries disappear! *Note:* If you have no coconut liqueur use Cream of Coconut (obtainable from good food stores). Use one measure to a half measure of dark rum.

GOLDEN GATE

☆ ☆ ☆

1 measure dark rum
1 measure gin
¼ measure dark crème de cacao
¼ measure lemon juice
Pinch of ginger
Orange slice (garnish)

Place ice cubes in shaker, then add all ingredients in order listed. Shake well and strain into a short tumbler over ice. Decorate with a slice of orange. This rich drink is very warming and deceptively easy to drink.

COFFEE/CHOCOLATE LIQUEUR COCKTAILS

FRUIT LIQUEURS

These are favourite drinks in both Europe and the United States. The American domestic cordials tend to be less subtle in flavour than their European counterparts, and less expensive. This is partly because the American versions are often made with artificial flavourings and sweeteners rather than fresh or dried fruit and other ingredients.

One notable flavour which is both a delightful drink served alone and an essential aid to making cocktails and cooking, is orange.

Orange and lemon peels are used as the flavourings for many liqueurs giving them an aromatic and slightly bitter taste which is offset by the sweetening added. Traditional orange liqueur, often made in Holland, is called *Curacao*. It is usually tinted brown, but may be clear or even blue in colour.

But the real winner for mixed drinks is colourless **Triple Sec**, a type of orange liqueur which is delicately flavoured and versatile. The best-known European brand of Triple Sec is *Cointreau,* but it is made by many companies.

Another bestseller in the American market is **Grand Marnier**, which includes real French cognac in its ingredients, and is caramel-coloured. It has a rich smooth flavour with a pungent aroma of orange. This liqueur and the white Triple Sec are invaluable in your home bar, with perhaps one of the unusual colours of curacao as a novelty.

Rock and Rye is a traditional American recipe which marries whiskey with citrus fruits. Rock candy is used to sweeten. Many companies make this liqueur, including *Donigan's, Arrow* and *De Kuyper*.

Another American favourite is **Southern Comfort**, which is aged in oak barrels to give a flavour of bourbon whiskey. It includes peach liqueur and extracts from fresh peaches. This is ideal over ice or in mixed drinks. Imitators of the style include *Yukon Jack* from Canada and *Laredo*.

Not peaches but apricots are the main flavour of another important international brand: *Amaretto di Saronno*. Beautifully presented, this fragrant liqueur is said to have been created by a young widow for her lover in the Italian town of Saronno. The style is much imitated but it is well worth seeking out the original. It is made with fresh apricot pulp and the kernels, which give an almond flavour to the drink.

Cherry Brandy is a British standard, offered to guests in country houses as they leave to go hunting on icy mornings.

Top brands of this rich and warming drink include *Peter Heering*, made in Denmark; *Cherry Marnier* from France sold in a lovely velvet-covered bottle; and *Grant's Cherry Brandy*, a renowned British brand. Other good names to look for include *De Kuyper* and *Bols*.

Soft fruits are also a base for some delightful liqueurs, such as **Crème de Cassis** from the Burgundy region of France and **Blackberry Cordial**, a traditional American choice.

Exotic fruits liqueurs are starting to gain popularity, especially the *Midori* melon liqueurs from Japan, with their bright green colour and unusual flavour. Banana liqueur, usually bright yellow, is strong in flavour and should be used sparingly, but it is excellent with desserts.

From Hawaii come rare specialities such as pineapple and passion fruit cordials. Ideal gifts if you are returning from a vacation there?

APRICOT LADY

☆ ☆

1 measure apricot liqueur
1 measure white rum
½ measure curacao orange
    liqueur
½ measure lime juice
Lime slice (garnish)
Fresh apricot (optional)

Place ice cubes in shaker, then
add all ingredients and shake
woll; ctrain into a tall tumblor ovor
crushed ice. Garnish with a lime
slice and fresh apricot if available.

COPENHEERING

☆ ☆

1 ½ measures Peter Heering
    cherry liqueur
½ measure gin
Cherry (garnish)

Shake liqueur and gin together
with ice, then strain into a cocktail
glass. This very pretty drink may
then be garnished witih a cocktail
cherry.

RHETT BUTLER

☆ ☆

1 measure Southern Comfort
1 measure curacao orange
*   liqueur*
Juice of ½ lime

Place ice cubes in shaker, then add all ingredients and shake well. Strain into a tall tumbler over crushed ice for a refreshing long drink.

SOUTHERN PEACH

☆ ☆

1 measure Southern Comfort
1 measure peach liqueur
Dash Angostura bitters
1 measure cream
Fresh peach and mint sprig
*   (garnish)*

Place ice cubes in shaker, then shake all ingredients well. This makes a thick "milkshake" texture which is delicious on a hot day. Serve either in a cocktail glass or a short tumbler over crushed ice. Garnish with a sliced fresh peach and a sprig of mint.

BLUE ANGEL

 ☆ ☆

1 measure blue curacao
1 measure grape brandy
Dash of lemon juice
Measure of thick cream

Like the Southern Peach this makes a drink with a thick, glossy texture which is lovely to look at. Place ice cubes in shaker and then add all ingredients and shake well; strain into a cocktail glass.

MIDORI TROPICAL

 ☆

1 measure Midori melon liqueur
2 measures orange juice
2 measures pineapple juice

Pour ingredients into a tall tumbler filled with crushed ice in order listed. Stir gently, then serve. Garnish with a fresh pineapple slice or orange slice as available.

SILVER JUBILEE

 ☆ ☆

1 measure crème de banane
  liqueur
1 measure gin
1 measure cream

Shake ingredients well with ice in a shaker, then strain into a cocktail glass. This is a grown-up banana milkshake!

HERBAL LIQUEURS

These are some of the world's oldest drinks, originally medicines prepared by monks in the Middle Ages. Today many are still made from ancient recipes. Perhaps the most famous of these herbal liqueurs are **Chartreuse** and **Benedictine**, both made in France and named after the order of monks who first prepared this special drink. Preparation of these liqueurs is a complex business and includes anything up to 30 different herbs and spices such as angelica, coriander, nutmeg, thyme and cardamom.

In Britain Scotch whisky is the base for a well-known herbal liquour, with a special taste of honey – **Drambuie**. This successful brand has encouraged a host of imitations, including *Glayva, Lochan Ora, Glen Mist* and *Loch Lomond*. In Ireland there is *Irish Mist*, naturally based on Irish, not Scotch, whiskey.

American whiskey, too, is used in the making of cordials such as **Yukon Jack, Wild Turkey** and **Jeremiah Weed**.

From Italy come some popular liqueurs which are used in many cocktails and served alone after dinner. These include **Strega**, which means "witch" in Italian; **Galliano**, a major ingredient in the Harvey Wallbanger cocktail; and **Sambuca**, which has an anise flavour and is usually served with roasted coffee beans floating on its surface. Try lighting the beans as you serve to give a very special aromatic and spectacular effect.

Herbal liqueurs are meant to aid digestion, and traditionally both caraway and mint were favourite indigestion remedies. **Kummel**, made in Germany and Holland, has caraway as a principal ingredient, and is a delicious after-dinner drink, served ice-cold in tiny glasses.

Mint is, of course, the major ingredient in **Crème de Menthe**, a firm favourite worldwide, which may be offered in clear, golden or green styles. Every U.S. cordial maker offers their own version, and it is interesting to compare some of the well-known European brands such as *Piperment Get, Cusenier Freezomint* and *Marie Brizard Crème de Menthe*. Serve Crème de Menthe over ice for a delicious *Crème de Menthe Frappée*; use cracked ice for extra effect. Mint is also used in the making of *peppermint schnapps*, a light style of American liqueur which is less rich than the European mint liqueurs.

SPRING COCKTAIL

☆ ☆

1 measure green Chartreuse
1 measure gin
Juice of ½ lemon

Place ice cubes in shaker and then add all ingredients; shake well and strain into a cocktail glass. This cocktail is a stunning colour!

WITCH'S POTION

☆

1 cup tea (hot)
1 measure Strega

Simply pour the Strega into the tea and allow the fumes to rise and clear your head. This is said to do wonders for a headache, but would make a reviving drink at any time.

EMBASSY

$\overline{Y}$ OR ☐   ☆ ☆

1 measure Drambuie
1 measure bourbon
½ measure sweet vermouth

Pour both ingredients slowly into
a cocktail glass or small tumbler.
Serve without ice as a "winter
warmer."

EMBASSY

$\overline{Y}$ OR ☐   ☆ ☆

1 measure Drambuie
1 measure bourbon
½ measure sweet vermouth

Pour ingredients slowly into
a cocktail glass or small tumbler.
Serve without ice as a "winter
warmer."

BITTERS

These drinks are direct descendants of herbal medicines prepared long ago by monks. Today they still have some beneficial properties; indeed, in the United States some bitters are classified as "medicinal" and sold in pharmacies. Other brands are described as "non-medicinal" and sold in liquor stores. Yet even these may be helpful for digestive upsets, particularly those caused by over-indulgence in food and drink!

Some bitters, including **Underberg** and **Fernet Branca**, both made in Europe, are meant to be served straight in tiny glasses as a "pick me up." In flavour, both of these fiery drinks are aptly called "bitters." Fernet Branca, from Italy, also has a mint version called *Branca Menta* with a slightly more agreeable taste than the original.

Also from Italy comes **Campari**, with its clear red colour and distinctive flavour. It is fast becoming a favourite base for a wide variety of cocktails, and certainly does not have a "cure" image. It may even be purchased in attractive miniature bottles, already mixed with soda.

In Britain and the United States **Angostura Bitters** are the favoured brand, and they are used in dozens of mixed drinks, as well as in cooking. Their flavour can also be used as a substitute for salt.

In France **Amer Picon** is an important brand, often served with ice and water. It includes brandy in its ingredients. Another common component of bitters is gentian root, and some French drinks are promoted as "gentian aperitifs." The major brand is **Suze**, a bright yellow in colour, with a powerful, almost harsh taste. Served with ice and soda it does stimulate the taste buds.

There are many American brands of bitters, several made in the style of Angostura Bitters. **Abbott's Aged Bitters** have been made by a family firm since 1865; **Peychaud Bitters** are made in New Orleans.

ANISEED DRINKS

Most countries of Europe have their own drinks based on aniseed, a traditional remedy for indigestion and a very refreshing flavour in hot weather. The styles range from *anisette*, which is a clear, sweet liqueur made in France by such companies as *Marie Brizard*, through **pastis**, which is dry and usually served with ice water, to various lower-alcohol brands such as *Pernod Light*, which is only 40 U.S. proof. Finally there are aniseed "cordials" which contain no alcohol at all, but are used to flavour water as a soft drink.

The ancestor of most of these is *absinthe*, made with wormwood and aniseed in the 19th century. It gained a reputation as a very dangerous and addictive tipple, and eventually production was banned during World War I. Some brands were sold then at around 130 proof, but the current aniseed drinks are around 70-80 U.S. proof. **Pernod** is sold worldwide, used in mixed drinks or served with ice and water (about 7 to 1 water is recommended). *Ricard* is a rival brand which is drier in flavour, a typical *pastis*.

In Greece they have **ouzo**, similar to pastis, in Spain it is **ojen**; in Italy **anesone**; and in Turkey **raki**. Puerto Rico produces a similar drink called **Tres Castillos**.

PINK GIN

☆ ☆

2 measures Plymouth gin (or London Dry)
5 drops Angostura bitters

Chill the cocktail glass and the gin before use. There are two ways of making this drink, according to whether you want to retain the bitters flavour or not. The first way, with "bitters out," is to place the drops of bitters in the glass, swirl them around, then pour them out. The gin is then added, and stirred very gently. Alternatively, pour in the gin, then add the bitters and stir gently. This traditional drink of the British Navy is said to ward off seasickness.

STOMACH REVIVER

☆ ☆

1 measure brandy
1 teaspoon Angostura bitters
½ measure Kummel
1 teaspoon Fernet Branca

Place ice cubes in shaker, then add all ingredients and shake well. Strain into a cocktail glass. Another recipe for fighting queasiness!

STEADIER

☆

1 measure brandy
2 dashes curacao (orange liqueur)
2 dashes Angostura bitters
Twist of lemon peel

Chill a cocktail glass, then add ingredients in order listed. Stir and serve with a twist of lemon peel. This one is said to steady the nerves.

113

TIGER TAIL

 ☆ ☆

2 measures Pernod
4 measures orange juice

Be sure orange juice is well chilled. Pour Pernod into tall tumbler, then add the juice. Stir and add ice if desired.

MORNING GLORY

 ☆ ☆

2 measures whiskey
2 dashes Pernod
Juice of 1 lime
1 ½ teaspoons castor sugar
1 egg white
Soda water (add last)

Put all ingredients except soda into blender and blend well for 20 seconds. Pour into a tall tumbler and add soda water to taste. A powerful but very refreshing brunch drink. Garnish with lime slice.

CARDINAL

☆ ☆

2 measures gin
4-5 drops Campari
2 dashes dry vermouth
Twist of lemon peel

A typically Italian drink – simply
stir all ingredients in a wine glass,
then garnish with the lemon peel.

HEMINGWAY

☆ ☆ ☆

1 measure Pernod
2 measures champagne (or
   sparkling wine)

Pour in Pernod to stemmed wine
glass, then add champagne or
sparkling wine to taste. This is
said to have been
a favourite of
Ernest Hemingway when he
lived in Paris.

There is a wine for all occasions. More and more people today are offering wines as a very acceptable alternative to the traditional cocktail, and, of course, wine is almost an essential for a good dinner. There is no secret to choosing suitable wines. Unfortunately a mystique surrounds the subject but the main points to remember are that certain wines are drier than others and that it is worth keeping both red and white wines in your home bar.

The simple difference between red and white wines is that the white wines are made from the juice of the grape alone, while red are made with the skins. This means that red wines have a certain harsh quality when they are young, often called astringency. Exceptions to this rule are Beaujolais wines from France, and certain California wines, which are made by a new process called carbonic maceration. This difference between red and white is why white wines are generally far superior as "cocktails" while red wines accompany full-flavoured foods to perfection.

The way to distinguish between table wines and fortified wines is easy. Look at the alcohol content. Fortified wines, usually contain about 20 per cent G.L. alcohol, while table wines are only about 11-13 per cent, although some full California wines may be more powerful. Of course, this alcohol content means that table wines are lower in calories as well, an important point for any dieters.

A BASIC WINE CELLAR
Not every home has a true cellar, and it is only fine wines that need special treatment. Everyday drinking wines need only a rack so that they can be stored lying down (to prevent the cork drying out) and temperature conditions that do not vary too much. A range from 55-75° Fahrenheit is acceptable. Bright light can also affect wines.

What to include in your own "cellar"? Start by assembling a basic collection of just one or two cases of wine (a case contains twelve bottles). If you generally drink wine with meals or as an "aperitif" before the meal you may like to invest in some of the new box wines which reduce storage space and are convenient. However, do check prices when buying; compare the price per litre with a wine in bottles and you may well find that the bottled wine is no more expensive.

Balance your selection like this:
DRY WHITE WINES
Choose Italian Frascati; French Muscadet, Chablis or Sancerre; Portuguese Vinho Verde; or California Fumé Blanc (4 × 75 cl. bottles)
FRUITY WHITE WINES
French white Burgundy, Vouvray, Alsace Sylvaner; Italian Soave or Orvieto; California or South African Colombard; Australian Semillon (4 × 75 cl. bottles)

MEDIUM-DRY WHITE WINES
German Rhine or Mosel; California Riesling; Yugoslav Riesling;
California Chenin Blanc (4 × 75 cl. bottles)
LIGHT RED WINES
French Beaujolais; Italian Valpolicella and Chianti; California Gamay
(4 bottles)
MEDIUM RED WINES
French Bordeaux ("claret"); Spanish Rioja; California Zinfandel;
Portuguese Dao wines (2/3 bottles)
FULL RED WINES
French Burgundy and Rhone wines; Italian Barbera wines; Australian
Shiraz; California Cabernet Sauvignon and Petite Syrah; Hungarian
"Bull's Blood" (2/3 bottles)
"FUN" WINES
Portuguese rosé; Italian Lambrusco; California rosé (2/3 bottles)

USING YOUR CELLAR

You will find that in general more white wine is served than red. Many
people do not drink red wine at all, and, of course, white wine is useful
for mixed drinks and as an aperitif alone, served chilled. If you
appreciate wine you will gradually add more good red wine for your
own use at dinner but with entertaining in mind consider the "fun
wines" which are ideal at parties.

WINE GADGETS

Decanters of all shapes and sizes are available for wine, although very
few wines need decanting. However, an ordinary red table wine (e.g.
California Burgundy) can benefit from airing for an hour or two in a
carafe or decanter, and, of course, the decanter is more attractive than
the bottle for serving at table. As a general rule, if you have any red wine
of more than ten years old do not decant for longer than two hours
unless your wine merchant says it is an exceptional vintage. White
wines do not need decanting.

When transferring wine to a decanter simply pour slowly and
steadily near a bright source of light. Once you can see a trace of
sediment rising to the neck of the bottle stop pouring.

When choosing a **corkscrew** look for one which is strongly made
and has a wire-type screw not the thick "gimlet" variety which can
make a mess of the cork. Do not use the type of corkscrew which
works with pumped air – this could spoil your wine.

Wine glasses should always be made with clear glass (except for
certain traditional German and Alsace styles) and have a stem so that
you can appreciate the colour of the wine and not transfer unwanted
heat to the wine. A "tulip" shape is considered ideal but do not select
the largest size as the fragrance of the wine can disappear in a large
goblet. White wines are traditionally offered in smaller glasses than red.
Ideally, you should "swirl" red wines and allow them to "breathe" and
release their aroma.

WINE WITH FOOD

Wine has digestive properties and actually makes food taste better,
apart from the pleasant effect of the alcohol. There is a wine to suit
every meal from informal picnics to elaborate receptions.

Before the meal, offer a light dry white wine, a glass of champagne
or perhaps a vermouth or glass of sherry. With the food, it is usual to

progress from light, dry wines to heavier fuller styles. So you could suggest a dry white wine with a fish first-course, or perhaps a rosé if it is paté or a light salad. With the main dish, red wine traditionally accompanies meats, and white wine, fish. With game you should choose one of the heavier red wines.

But these rules are not hard and fast, and some fish dishes, such as Italian *cioppino* with its rich stock, are ideal with light red wine. White meats, too, are excellent with a medium-bodied white wine. A red wine could overpower the delicate flavour. The same is true of chicken and turkey dishes, although claret (French Bordeaux wine) is traditional with a British Christmas turkey dinner. An American equivalent would be California Cabernet Sauvignon.

Cheeses marry perfectly with wine, and the smooth qualities of cheese actually improve a rather harsh red wine. Choose a full red wine to accompany most cheeses, although goat's cheese is good with French white Burgundy or California Chardonnay.

With dessert, offer a German Riesling or perhaps a South African Steen wine. There are also special dessert wines, rich and sweet, which could be "bought in" to add to your cellar for a special event. These include French *Sauternes* and *Barsac* and California *Moscato Amabile*, which is also made in Italy.

After the meal the choice is wide; some guests who are diet-conscious might enjoy another glass of medium white wine as a "digestif." Or those who like a fuller flavour would appreciate a glass of rich red port.

KIR

1 measure dry white wine
1 teaspoon crème de cassis
(black currant liqueur)

Use a small wine glass and chill
first. Pour in the liqueur and then
add wine to taste. This is a
traditional drink in Burgundy and
very attractive to look at, as well
as low in calories.

MULLED WINE

4 measures dry red wine
3 cloves
Cinnamon stick
Twist of lemon peel
1 teaspoon castor sugar
1 dash Angostura bitters
1 pinch allspice

Heat all the ingredients gently in a
pot on the stove but do not allow
to boil. Pour into mugs or glasses
with a spoon in to prevent
cracking. Stir with a cinnamon
stick as garnish.

SANGRIA

⛾ ☆

1 bottle Spanish full red wine or
California Zinfandel
Juice of a lemon and an orange
Three sliced fresh oranges
Half-cup of castor sugar

Put all ingredients into a punch
bowl with ice or an ice block. Stir
gently, then add soda as
required. Serve garnished with an
orange slice.

SPRITZER

🍷 ☆

1 glass dry white wine
4 measures soda or sparkling
mineral water
Lime slice (garnish)

Pour wine into glass then twist
lime slice into the wine – add
mineral water or soda to taste.
Garnish with the lime slice.
Marvellous on hot days.

121

FORTIFIED WINE

APPETIZER & DESSERT WINES

Apart from table wines, which are enjoying such success at present, there is another style of wine which has been popular over many years. These are the **fortified** wines, which are made by adding just a little spirit (often brandy) so that they have a richer, fuller flavour and are higher in alcoholic strength than dry table wines. A typical fortified wine would be about 40 U.S. proof as opposed to 25-30 proof for a light table wine.

Perhaps the most famous of all fortified wines, and certainly one of the most versatile, is **vermouth.** There are various styles of vermouth available, including the delicately-flavoured dry white style, traditionally called "French," although it is also made in Italy and other countries of the world. The classic "Italian" style is a sweet red vermouth with a full herbal flavour. Between these extremes are a medium-dry white version, often called *Bianco* in Italy (the sweet style is called *Rosso*), and now a relatively new rose version, which has gained popularity in recent years and is also medium-dry. All vermouths may be served alone, over ice with a twist of lemon, or in a wide variety of mixed drinks.

Sherry is a favourite drink in Britain, and becoming more popular in the United States. True sherry must be made around the Jerez district of Spain, but similar drinks are also made in Cyprus, South Africa and California. When choosing Spanish sherry, make sure that you are purchasing the type you prefer. They range from very dry to extremely sweet. The driest of all is *Manzanilla*, said to have the salty tang of the sea near the vineyards where it is made. Next comes *Fino*, also very pale in colour, and light and dry. Both of these should be served cool. The most popular sherry in Britain is *Amontillado*, golden in colour and medium-dry in taste. For those with an inclination toward sweeter drinks, choose a fine *Oloroso* or *Amoroso* for a subtle and complex flavour, or a *Cream* sherry, such as the famous *Harvey's Bristol Cream*, which may also be served as a dessert wine. Apart from Harvey's, other well-known Spanish sherry shippers include *Gonzalez Byass* and *Domecq*.

Madeira was the favoured drink of the early American settlers and George Washington often enjoyed a glass with his meals. This wine has a pungent flavour which comes from having been heated in a special "hot house" known as an *estufa*. Then brandy is added and the maderia is blended before bottling. The various styles of madeira available today are named after the grape varieties used in their making: *Sercial* is a light dry style, often served cool; *Verdelho* has a pale gold colour and is served cool; *Bual* is medium-sweet and offered with or without ice; and *Malmsey* has a full gold colour and is the sweetest of all. Famous shippers of Madeira include *Cossart Gordon* and *Rutherford*.

Port is another rich drink favoured by the British on long winter days and evenings. It is made by adding brandy to good quality Portuguese red wine. In the past, the brandy helped to preserve the wine during long sea voyages. True port is still made in Portugal around the town of Oporto, but fair imitations are now made in Australia, South Africa and California. Port is aged in wood casks before shipment and described according to colour and age: *Ruby* port is younger and usually less expensive; *Tawny* port has taken on a brown tinge from the wood and may well cost more. *Vintage* port is very heavy and rich in style – a drink for the connoisseur. It is only made in years when the grapes are of exceptional quality, and should be kept for at least ten years from the date on the bottle before drinking. Well-known port shippers include *Dow, Warre, Taylor, Sandeman* and *Cockburn*. In California, *Paul Masson* and *Fickling* make a good local "port."

Other sweet fortified wines include **Marsala** from Sicily in Italy, which is often used in cooking and may be offered as a dessert wine. Sometimes egg is added to it, and it is then called *Marsala all'uovo*. **Tokay** is the name of a legendary sweet wine form Hungary which has been made for hundreds of years. It is not fortified. Today, however, only tiny quantities of Tokay are made, but in the United States a drink of the same name is prepared from California port, a pale fortified wine made from white grapes, and angelica.

Muscatel wines are made all over the world from the sweet muscat grapes. Not all are fortified and some are sweet if the grapes themselves were extremely ripe when picked. Pale Muscatels are often made from Muscat of Alexandria grapes, and the darker styles from Black Muscat grapes.

HOW TO SERVE FORTIFIED WINES

In the past, all fortified wines were served at room temperature. Their superior alcoholic strength made them ideal "winter warmers." Today, there are still some which should never be offered over ice, such as fine vintage port. Allow it to breathe before serving as you would a fine red wine. Similarly, the sweeter sherries and madeiras are very pleasant when served at room temperature after a meal.

But the majority of these drinks are excellent when chilled or served with ice. The light sherries such as *fino* should be served in small glasses, known as *copitas*, which are like small tulip-shaped wine glasses. Chill the bottle before serving, but ice is not necessary as it tends to dilute the flavour of the drink. Medium sherries and most madeiras are agreeable when served with ice in a wine goblet, as are all the various styles of vermouth. And, of course, there are many mixed drinks based on vermouth.

In the kitchen fortified wines play an important role. A little medium sherry added to beef consommé, for instance, makes all the difference in flavour. And making *zabaglione* would be impossible without marsala. Vermouth may be added to many sweet and savoury recipes, especially those with an Italian origin. Lovers of Stilton cheese find it much improved if a little is scooped out of the centre and a glass of port added and allowed to soak into the cheese. Similarly a glass of rich port is a lovely way to fill a half-melon as an appetizer or dessert.

Madeira and sherry

CORONATION

☆ ☆

1 measure dry sherry
1 measure dry vermouth
1 dash Maraschino (liqueur)
2 dashes Angostura bitters
3 measures medium white wine
Soda water to top up
Mint sprig (garnish)

Mix with ice in a mixing glass,
adding ingredients in order of
listing. Then transfer into a tall
tumbler and top with soda to
taste. Decorate with mint.

CHRISTMAS WASSAIL
PUNCH

☆

4 bottles medium sherry
1 pound sugar
1 teaspoon powdered nutmeg
2 teaspoons powdered ginger
6 whole allspice
1 teaspoon cinnamon
½ pint water
12 eggs, separated
12 apples

First, bake the apples in a
moderate oven (350°F) for about
30 minutes. Then put all
ingredients except sherry and
eggs into a saucepan and mix
well. Add the sherry and heat
gently. Beat the egg yolks and
add to the mixture (away from
heat), then whisk the egg whites
and stir in. Finally, float the baked
apples on top and
serve in generous
punch cups.

PORT IN A STORM

2 measures ruby port
2 dashes brandy
Juice of ½ lemon

Pour all ingredients over ice in a mixing glass and stir well. Then strain into a cocktail glass to serve. The tartness of the lemon cuts through the richness of the port to make a very pleasant light drink.

SHERRY FLIP

2 measures medium sherry
1 teaspoon castor sugar
1 egg
4 dashes crème de cacao liqueur
Nutmeg

Put all ingredients except nutmeg into blender and blend well with ½ cup cracked ice. Pour into frosted cocktail glasses and sprinkle with nutmeg.

BERETTA

♀ OR ☐ ♂ ☆ ☆ ☆

1 measure dry vermouth
½ measure gin
2 measures orange curaçao
3 measures medium white wine
2 dashes Angostura bitters
Orange slice (garnish)

Mix all ingredients in a mixing glass with ice, then pour into a large wine goblet or short tumbler to serve, with or without ice as preferred. Garnish with orange slice.

EAST AND WEST

☐ ☐ ☆ ☆

½ measure port
½ measure brandy
½ measure orange curaçao
¼ measure lemon juice
Orange and lemon slices
  (garnish)

Shake ingredients well with ice and strain into a short tumbler with some crushed ice. Garnish with orange and lemon slices.

GREENBRIAR

 ☆ ☆ ☆

2 measures dry sherry
1 measure dry vermouth
1 dash Angostura bitters

Mix ingredients well with ice in a
mixing glass and then pour into a
short tumbler. Add ice cubes if
desired and garnish with fresh
mint sprig.

LIGHT 'N' DRY

☆ ☆

1 measure dry sherry
½ measure brandy
½ measure light rum
1 dash Angostura bitters

Stir ingredients with ice in a
mixing glass. Strain into a cocktail
glass. Top with crushed ice if
desired. No garnish necessary.

CHAMPAGNE

Although most people tend to think of all sparkling wines as
"champagne" in fact only a tiny proportion of these wines are actually
made in the Champagne region of France, and are therefore entitled to
bear the proud original name. But the others are often just as drinkable,
and far less expensive. True champagne is sold in a variety of styles, all
with the special "toasty" flavour which is the characteristic of this
famous celebration drink. *Brut* champagne is dry and crisp, while *Extra
Dry* or *Demi-Sec* are medium dry (despite the name). Then there is
vintage champagne, made only in fine quality years, and sold at high
prices. It is a great shame to add anything to vintage champagne,
which should be served in lovely glasses and enjoyed sip by sip.

However, there are many delightful mixed drinks made with
champagne which may just as well be prepared with an alternative
sparkling wine. The choice of sparkler can be confusing. In general, it is
best to avoid the very cheapest sparkling wine. It may have been made
with poor quality grapes and have rather a dull, insipid flavour. Look for
a wine made by the *méthode champenoise*, if available. This means
that it has been made by the same process as "true" champagne,
which yields a more subtle flavour and more persistent "mousse" or
bubbles. Those durable bubbles are important when mixing sparkling
wine. You will not enjoy a Champagne Cocktail which is flat!

Incidentally, remember never to mix up any concoction with
sparkling wine in your blender. The consequence could be a
re-decorated kitchen or bar, as the bubbles will create a near-
explosion. Use a shaker or a mixing glass as recommended. Another
item of equipment to be avoided is the "swizzle stick." These were
popular in the 1930s, when some people believed that the bubbles
upset the stomach. In truth, it is the alcohol which could disturb your
digestion, so if that is your problem you might prefer drinking one of the
non-alcoholic cocktails at the end of this book. But for the rest of us,
why not appreciate the beauty of a delicately-tinted sparkling cocktail,
attractively served? If the fizz makes you feel a little light-headed, well,
that is the idea of a celebration drink.

A GUIDE TO BRANDS

When choosing a bottle of real champagne for a special occasion, it is
usually safest to look for one of the well-known brands, known as the
"grandes marques." Perhaps the most famous of all is *Moet et
Chandon*, who distribute their various bottlings worldwide, and also
own *Mercier* and *Ruinart*. Their most expensive offering is *Dom
Perignon*, named after the monk who is said to have invented the
champagne method. This is a deluxe bottle with only the finest quality
selected vats or *cuvées* used in its preparation, and the price reflects
its rarity.

For those who like a full, rich taste when they drink champagne, try
Bollinger, a favourite of the British Royal Family; or *Krug*, with its lovely
swan-necked bottles. Lighter styles with a tarter taste include *Lanson*
and *Laurent Perrier*. *Taittinger* is also widely available, and they sell a

lovely light champagne made only with selected white grapes, a *blanc de blanc* – it is called *Comtes de Champagne.* Other names to look for include *Pol Roger, Charles Heidsieck* and *Joseph Perrier.* You can also ask your wine merchant for a recommendation. He may stock a "house" choice which offers sound value for money but does not have a famous name.

Alternatives to champagne include some excellent wines made in Spain, France and Italy, as well as California and Australia. In France, they make fine-quality sparkling wine around the Saumur region in the Loire Valley. Names to look for include *Ackerman Laurance* and *Gratien Meyer*; in Burgundy a well-known local sparkling wine is called *Kriter.*

Spanish sparkling wine is almost all made by the proper *méthode champenoise* and makes an inexpensive alternative to French wines. Look for *Cava, Freixenet* or *Codorniu* on the label to ensure a reliable selection.

In Italy, sparkling wine is made both sweet and dry, but perhaps their best example is *Asti Spumante* which has the aroma of muscat grapes and is delicious with dessert. It is not suitable for mixed drinks because its flavour is too pungent.

In America, the finest "champagnes" are made in California, and brands such as *Schramsberg* and *Korbel* have worldwide reputations. New York State, too, is a source of some sparkling wines which mix well in cocktails. Look for *Taylor, Great Western* and *Gold Seal. Great Western* is also a notable name for Australian sparkling wine made by the large firm of *Seppelt.*

HOW TO SERVE CHAMPAGNE & SPARKLING WINES

When serving any sparkling wine, either alone or as a mixed drink, the choice of glass is very important. Try to banish the image of the traditional "coupe" shape of glass and think instead of a tall, slim glass, perhaps with a slight inward tulip-shaped curve at the top. The traditional glass may look pretty but its shape allows the bubbles to escape very rapidly and the pleasure of drinking a sparkling wine is lost. The tall shape preserves the fizz and also shows off a mixed champagne cocktail to perfection. Of course, for a cocktail which contains spirits as well as champagne it is perfectly logical to use a Martini-style cocktail glass, or even a short tumbler.

Serve sparkling wine well-chilled, but not too cold. A good way of achieving the correct temperature is to chill the bottle in your refrigerator and then remove it about a half hour before serving. Transfer the bottle to an ice bucket filled with ice and water. This will slightly reduce the chill on the bottle and keep it at precisely the right temperature for drinking. To open a bottle of sparkling wine, first wrap a napkin around the neck of the bottle to catch any stray drops. Then carefully undo the metal wire holding the cork. Place a glass nearby for the first few ounces of wine. Be sure you are holding the cork firmly to avoid any accidents (never aim a cork anywhere near anything breakable!). Twist the bottle gently until the cork slips free with a faint hiss, not a loud bang – twisting the cork is a risky business because it might break and need a corkscrew to remove it, a lengthy and embarrassing procedure for you. Each bottle will serve about six glasses of champagne.

CHAMPAGNE COCKTAIL

 ☆

1 cube sugar
1 dash Angostura bitters
Twist of lemon peel
Champagne

Put the sugar lump in a tall glass or cocktail glass and add the bitters and the twist of lemon peel. With a small spoon, crush the sugar very gently to allow bitters to be absorbed. Then pour on the champagne to taste. Use real champagne for this drink if you can afford it.

BELLINI

☆

1 measure fresh peach juice
   (fresh-squeezed, if possible)
1 dash grenadine, if desired
Champagne

Pour in peach juice to a tall wine glass, add grenadine if desired, then top with well-chilled champagne or Italian sparkling wine (dry). This delicious cocktail was invented in Venice and is very popular there.

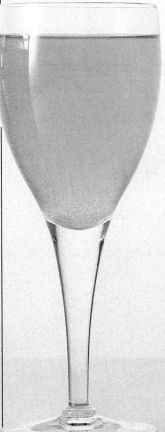

CHAMPAGNE MIXED DRINKS

BLUE CHAMPAGNE

 ☆

*4 dashes blue curacao (orange
    liqueur)
1 orange slice
Champagne or sparkling wine*

Swirl the curacao around the
sides of a tall wine glass or
cocktail glass. Pour in
champagne or sparkling wine to
taste and then add the orange
slice as garnish. A drink with the
most unusual colour, this is also
an attractive flavour combination.

BUCKS' FIZZ or MIMOSA

 ☆

*2 measures fresh, chilled orange
    juice
1 dash grenadine, if desired
Champagne*

This refreshing drink may be
made with either fine
champagne, in which case it is
called *Bucks' Fizz,* or with
California champagne, which is a
Mimosa. For either drink, simply
pour the orange juice into a
goblet or short tumbler and top
with chilled sparkling wine. The
grenadine is optional, and adds a
little extra sweetness and colour.

134

AMERICANA

☆ ☆

1 measure bourbon whiskey
1 dash Angostura bitters
½ teaspoon castor sugar
Champagne
Peach slice to decorate

This is one drink which is agreeable in an old-fashioned champagne "coupe" glass – or use a cocktail glass. Stir the whiskey, sugar and bitters in a mixing glass, then pour into the serving glass and add champagne. Decorate with a peach slice.

KIR ROYALE

☆

Champagne
Dash of crème de cassis (black currant liqueur)

Pour the crème de cassis into a tall wine glass (a teaspoonful is all that is required), then add the champagne or top-quality sparkling wine. A simple yet irresistible drink, popular in the Champagne region of France.

BEER & CIDER

You may not consider beer or cider worthy occupants of your home bar especially if you associate them with football games and "serious drinking" away from home. But there are some very fine beers and ciders which demand attention both as thirst-quenching drinks and as individual taste sensations. Add to this the fact that beer and cider are both relatively low in calories and you have some powerful arguments in favour of stocking at least a few bottles or cans at home.

THE CHOICE OF BEERS
Like wines, beers may be divided into various categories. The "red wines" are heavier beers made by traditional methods, such as porters, stouts, old-fashioned British ales, and all-wheat beers, including those made in Germany and Belgium. By contrast, the "white wines" are noticeably paler in colour and lighter in flavour. These include the famous German Pilsener beers and all other world beers known as "lager."

In general, the lager style of beer is preferred for home drinking because it is easier to maintain in good condition, either in bottles or cans. In fact, the word lager means "store" in German, and refers to the three months maturation undergone by these beers before sale. By contrast, the heavier traditional ales tend to be served in specialist bars and clubs because they need careful storage and serving conditions to taste their best. Of course, there are exceptions to these general rules, such as bottled Guinness stout or some British ales which are specifically meant to be consumed at home.

The choice of brand can prove tricky now that there is such a vast range of imported beer available in off-licences. Price is obviously a basic guide, bearing in mind that imported Pilsener from Germany or Czechoslovakia will cost far more than domestic beer, but may not be appreciated more by your guests who simply crave a cool and refreshing drink. When choosing American beer look for the designation Premium or Super Premium on the label, meaning the beer is high quality. Reliable American brands include *Coors, Budweiser, Olympia, Pabst* and *Schlitz*. On the East Coast *Ballantine* and *Genesee* have good reputations.

Imported lagers which are easy to obtain, and light and agreeable to drink include *Heineken, Carlsberg, Diat Pils* and *Stella Artois*. Certain lagers such as *Diat Pils* do claim to be better for the calorie-conscious because they have less sugar than other brands. There are also some U.S. "lite" beers which are low-calorie.

Among the traditional ales, look for *Watneys, Courage* and *Trumans* on the world market. In Britain, *Fullers* and *Ruddles* are readily obtained and have the authentic taste of old-fashioned British ale. The styles to look for are *bitter* or *pale ale*, both of which are brown in colour and usually served lukewarm in Britain (cellar temperature). Heavier than these are the *stouts* and *porters* of which the most famous worldwide is Irish *Guinness*, a truly black beer with a distinctive rich and bitter flavour. In California, there is an excellent porter made by the Anchor Steam Brewery, but this style is rare in the United States.

CIDER
There is a little difficulty in defining cider in America because non-alcoholic apple juice is often sold under this name in supermarkets. In Europe cider is definitely an alcoholic beverage, with about the same strength as beer (around 10 U.S. proof). Apples are fermented to make cider, as grapes are used in the making of wine, and malt and hops in the preparation of beer. The result is a full-flavoured and very refreshing drink, which is lovely with outdoor meals and during hot weather. Well-known British brands include *Merrydown*, *Taunton* and *Bulmers*, and there are also some fine ciders made in the Normandy region of France. Both the United States and Canada have many brands of domestic cider, and it is important to check the label for the degree of sweetness as well as the alcohol content when buying.

SERVING BEERS AND CIDERS
With the exception of some very strong ales and porters, these are light, fizzy drinks which benefit from chilling and serving cool. Choose attractive glass tankards or tall tumblers to show off the colour and appearance of these drinks. No garnish or ice is used for beers, but cider can be served with added sliced apple to emphasize the apple fragrance. Try using it when next "bobbing for apples" at Hallowe'en.

BLACK VELVET

½ glass champagne or sparkling
   wine
½ glass Guinness

Half fill a tall wine glass with
Guinness. Top up carefully with
champagne or sparkling wine.
Note: pour carefully to avoid the
drink becoming too lively and
wasting the sparkling wine!

SEKT SPARKLER

½ glass Sekt (German sparkling
   wine)
½ glass Pilsener (German lager
   beer)

Use a small beer tankard or large
wine goblet. Half fill with the lager
beer, then top with German or
similar sparkling wine (both well-
chilled).

LEMON TOP

Dry cider (still or sparkling)
Juice of 1 lemon

Pour the cider into a short or tall tumbler and then add the lemon juice. Do not stir but sip the cider through the juice to make a "sweet and sour" drink.

CIDER CUP

2 litres dry cider
2 measures Maraschino (cherry liqueur)
2 measures orange curacao (liqueur)
2 measures brandy

Pour all ingredients into a large glass jug or bowl. Add plenty of ice and stir gently. Decorate with sliced apple and orange. Serve in large wine glasses or punch cups.

MIXERS

While alcoholic drinks are the backbone of any home bar, they would not be sufficient alone to make an interesting range of drinks. To add variety, and to ensure your cocktails are not too overpowering, you need mixers of various kinds. Ready-made drinks mixers are available but while these are convenient when travelling, they are no substitute for mixing the separate ingredients of a drink in the exact proportions that you profor.

The most important mixers to keep at home are soda water (or mineral water); ginger ale; tonic water, cola; and a lemon or lime soda.

SODA WATER

Often known as Club Soda in the United States, this is the simplest yet most vital mixer of all. It is merely water with carbon dioxide gas added to give bubbles. Mixed with any spirit, it has the virtue of lengthening the drink without adding any detracting flavour. Combined with ice, soda makes almost any drink more "summery"' and refreshing. To give a notion of the many drinks made with soda, try Scotch and Soda, Campari and Soda, Brandy and Soda, Spritzer (wine with added soda) and even Fruit Juice with Soda! In addition, it is an essential added ingredient for all fruit punches, and for many cocktails, where it is poured in (or squirted through a soda syphon) at the last moment. A soda syphon can be a very useful additon to your home bar.

Apart from traditional soda, there is an interest these days in **mineral waters.** These are naturally-occurring spring waters from various parts of the world. Some have spontaneous "fizz" or added carbon dioxide bubbles. Use them in place of soda with any subtly-flavoured drink such as dry white wine for a really healthy and low-calorie drink. Well-known brands include *Perrier, Badoit* and *Spa* from Europe, *Malvern* and *Ashbourne* from Britain.

Sparkling water is available in syphons (with rechargeable cylinders) or in bottles. If you buy bottles, make sure you buy the right size so that the water is not left to go flat and wasted. Best of all, invest in a mixer-making machine such as the *Sodastream* which adds sparkle to ordinary drinking water and means you always have access to immediate soda water and other mixers as required.

Of course, there are some drinks which require simple unsparkling water. Examples include Scotch or Bourbon with water and anise drinks such as *Pernod* and *Ricard*, which are served with ice water. For these, offer iced water in an attractive glass or ceramic jug for guests to add as they please. Alternatively, you might open a bottle of still mineral water, said to be purer and more flavour-free than ordinary water.

GINGER ALE

In previous centuries, ginger was valued as an aid to digestion, and it certainly can still have a therapeutic effect when mixed with Scotch or brandy. There are two different styles available in Britain: Dry Ginger

Ale, which has a sharp taste, and American Ginger Ale, a sweeter and smoother version. Both are agreeable drinks alone or with spirits.

TONIC WATER
Like ginger ale, this began as a medicine. The early tonic water was made with quinine, a bitter-tasting extract which was highly effective in the treatment of malaria and other tropical diseases. In the days of Empire tonic water was mixed with London Dry Gin as an agreeable and useful drink in a hot climate, and this is still the most popular mix for this soda. However, it is also very pleasant when added to vodka or tequila, and it is an intriguing ingredient of many cocktails.

COLA
As tonic water is associated with the name of *Schweppes*, so cola is with *Coke* (Coca-Cola) and *Pepsi*. Again these were medicinal connections, as cocaine is said to have been included in the original blend and lent the drink its name. Today it is the world's most popular soft drink, rather too distinctive in flavour for mixing except with pungently flavoured spirits such as white rum – *Bacardi & Coke* is an example of two brand names passing into the language as a cocktail. With the new importance of low-calorie mixers, diet versions of cola are very popular with many people and are useful to have on hand.

LEMON/LIME SODA
In Britain, the popular drink lemonade is simply a fizzy mixer with citrus flavouring. But in the United States and elsewhere in the world, it is quite different, made with fresh lemon, sugar and water. If a lemon mixer is required, there are various brands of lemon and/or lime soda such as *Seven-Up* which are fairly dry and pleasant to drink. Other citrus fruits are sometimes used as in *Squirt* which has grapefruit juice as a major ingredient.

FRUIT JUICES
Most sparkling mixers contain either sugar or saccharin in their ingredients, and the low-calorie versions have artificial sweeteners. Some people feel that it is healthier and more interesting to drink fresh fruit juice, which is sold without added sweetening. One pleasant way to drink juice is mixed with sparkling mineral water, making a sparkling juice drink. Juices may also be mixed with one another in "cocktails" which are ideal for breakfast time. The major juices avilable include orange, grapefruit, tomato, pineapple and apple, and all have their place in the home bar, for serving alone or as mixers. Tomato juice is especially useful for anyone who cannot or chooses not to drink alcohol as it is a "savoury" drink which sharpens the appetite.

THE ALTERNATIVE COCKTAIL
It is always polite to offer guests an alternative to alcohol at any party, and these days there are many recipes for cocktails made with juice and mixers which look and taste almost as attractive as the real thing. Thse drinks are also good to serve at children's parties, when you can use the whole range of cocktail accessories such as paper umbrellas and straws to excellent effect. Many of the recipes already offered in this book may be readily adapted for this purpose simply by leaving out the spirit or wine base, but there are some blends specifically designed to please those who have to drink *and* drive.

KEEP SOBER

3 measures tonic water
½ measure grenadine syrup
   (made with pomegranates)
½ measure lemon syrup

Pour ingredients in order listed
into tall tumbler. Add ice to taste.

ST. CLEMENTS

2 measures orange juice
2 measures bitter lemon soda
Orange and lemon slices
   (garnish)

Chill ingredients before serving.
Stir with ice in a jug then, strain
into a tall tumbler. Add crushed
ice if liked and serve with a straw,
garnished with orange and lemon
slices.

SAN FRANCISCO

1 measure orange juice
1 measure lemon juice
1 measure pineapple juice
1 measure grapefruit juice
2 dashes grenadine
1 egg white
Soda water
Sliced citrus fruits (garnish)

Shake all the fruit juices, egg white and grenadine with ice in a shaker, then strain into a large wine goblet or short tumbler. Add soda water to taste and decorate with fruit slices, and a straw.

TENDERBERRY

1 measure dry ginger ale
1 measure thick cream
1 measure grenadine
6-8 strawberries
Ground ginger to taste

Put strawberries, grenadine and cream into the electric blender with some crushed ice. Blend on maximum speed for 30 seconds. Pour into a tumbler, then add dry ginger to taste and stir. Decorate with a fresh strawberry and serve with a straw.

PARSON'S SPECIAL

□ 🍸

2 measures orange juice
4 dashes of grenadine
1 egg yolk

Place ice cubes in shaker and
then add all ingredients; shake
well and strain into a short
tumbler. *Note:* this makes an eye-
opening breakfast drink.

LIMEY

🍸 🍸

1 measure lime juice
½ measure lemon juice
½ egg white

Shake the ingredients in a shaker
with ice cubes, then strain into a
cocktail glass. *Note:* Lime juice is
the reason the British are known
as "limeys" in the United States –
they drank juice on long sea
voyages to avoid scurvy and
other ills caused by vitamin
deficiency.

PUSSYFOOT

½ measure orange juice
½ measure lemon syrup
1 measure cola

Shake all ingredients well with ice
and then strain into a short
tumbler over ice. Decorate with
lemon slices if desired.

NURSERY FIZZ

2 measures orange juice
2 measures dry ginger ale

Fill a large wine glass with
crushed ice and then add the
juice and ginger ale. Decorate
with a cocktail cherry and an
orange slice. Serve with a straw.

146

JERSEY LILY

3 measures apple juice
2 dashes Angostura bitters
1/4 teaspoon castor sugar
 (optional)
Soda water or mineral water to
 top up
Cherry (garnish)

Stir the juice, bitters and sugar
well with ice in a mixing jug or
glass, then strain into a wine
glass. Top with sparkling soda or
water. *Note:* This drink may also
be made with sparkling apple
juice. Decorate with a cocktail
cherry.

CAFE ASTORIA

2 measures milk
1/4 measure pineapple juice
1/4 measure lemon juice
1/2 measure coffee essence
Chocolate vermicelli to decorate

Place all ingredients in goblet of
blender with crushed ice and
blend on maximum speed for 30
seconds. Pour into a cocktail
glass and sprinkle chocolate
vermicelli on top just before you
serve.

CARIB CREAM

1 measure lemon juice
1 measure milk
1 small banana, sliced
1 teaspoon chopped walnuts

Place sliced banana, milk and juice in the blender with crushed ice and blend on maximum speed until smooth. Pour into a cocktail glass and sprinkle walnuts on as you serve.

LEMONADE PUNCH

2 quarts strong tea
Juice of 6 lemons
1 cup castor sugar
1 quart of ginger ale
Sprigs of mint

Allow tea to cool before use, then add lemon juice, sugar and mint. Let this mixture marinate for about an hour before serving, then add ginger ale. Serve in tall glasses or punch cups and decorate with mint.

VIRGIN MARY

3 measures tomato juice
¼ measure lemon juice
Pinch of salt
Black pepper to taste
1 dash Worcestershire sauce
1 dash Tabasco
Celery salt (optional)
Celery stick (garnish)

Fill a tall tumbler half full of ice, then add ingredients in order listed. Stir gently with the celery stick, sprinkle with celery salt if liked and serve.

PRAIRIE OYSTER

2 teaspoons tomato juice
1 egg yolk
2 dashes wine vinegar
Black pepper to taste
1 teaspoon Worcestershire sauce
1 dash Tabasco

Put all ingredients but egg yolk in a wine glass. Stir gently then add yolk carefully to avoid breaking. Serve before breakfast to anyone feeling fragile!

149

PARTIES

With so many drinks to choose from, how are you to decide which to offer your guests on any particular occasion? Of course, personal taste will sometimes be your guide, but often you are in doubt about preferences and need a "menu" of drinks to appeal to all tastes.

THE CLASSIC COCKTAIL PARTY

There has been a revival of these lately, as the fashion for elegant cocktails returns. A well-balanced menu might include the following:

Dry Martini   **Dlack Nussian**
Singapore Gin Sling **Whiskey Sour**
Piña Colada

To this list, which covers the major spirits, you could add a **Tequila Sunrise** for guests who enjoy tequila, and one or two drinks based on wine, such as a **Kir** and a **Champagne Cocktail**. Try not to exceed a maximum of eight drinks, and draw up a full check list of all ingredients required for your bartender before the party. Be sure you have plenty of soft drinks for anyone who might prefer these, and, of course, you can mix these into an "alternative cocktail" as required.

When planning your cocktail party, think about how many guests you expect and buy accordingly. If serving wine, calculate that a typical bottle (75 cl. bottle) serves about six glasses. For spirits, a standard bottle (called a "fifth" in the U.S.) also contains 75 cl. and will serve 17 normal measures known as "jiggers." Roughly speaking, you should plan on 50 measures from three bottles of spirit, remembering that some of the mixed drinks in this book call for double measures. If you are saving money and buying by the case (12 bottles) plan on 200 measures per case.

In addition to the basic cocktail styles mentioned, remember to have plain soda available for those who like whiskey and soda, and a fortified wine such as sherry for those who do want a mixed drink, as well as white wine (dry) for anyone on a diet. Keep a good selection of mixers for anyone who chooses a drink without alcohol.

Designing an attractive card listing the cocktails is a useful time-saving idea and also a conversation opener as guests arrive. These drinks are fairly powerful and alcohol stimulates the appetite, so accompanying snacks could be fairly substantial Possible choices might include stuffed eggs with a touch of curry in the mayonnaise; cocktail sausages served in a chafing dish with barbecue sauce; cheese pastry puffs or anchovy puffs; or canapés. To make canapés, use day-old bread and fry it lightly in oil before use. Blot on paper towels then allow it to cool. You should remove the crust before covering with a spread. Cutting the fried bread into circles with a biscuit cutter makes a festive design. Spread with fillings as needed but try not to make too many as they become moist quickly. Try some of the following spreads: cream cheese with paprika and black olive garnish; scrambled eggs with a little smoked salmon; blue cheee blended with a little brandy; cream cheese with a little redcurrant or raspberry jelly.

Manhattan

Dry Martini

THE ALL-AMERICAN PARTY
If your team just completed a winning season, or for any celebration, why not plan a truly American cocktail party? Offer guests whiskey-based drinks such as the **Manhattan**, the **Old Fashioned**, the **Whiskey Sour**, and perhaps the **Mint Julep** if it is a hot day. Serve substantial canapés with this, such as tiny meatballs with spicy barbecue sauce, or stuffed eggs with plenty of mayonnaise mixed with egg yolk and sprinkled with cayenne pepper. Or use pastry to fashion *vol au vents* (also available ready to cook in supermarkets). Fill these with chicken and mayonnaise, cream cheese and celery, or tuna with spicy tomato sauce.

151

A WINE AND CHEESE PARTY

Here is an idea with infinite variations. Try featuring the wines of one country, or serve all white wines, if you plan an outdoor party. To keep the cost down and yet have the opportunity to try a variety of fine wines, some hosts suggest that guests bring a bottle, giving a clue as to the area or style of wine to be served. For a typical wine and cheese party, plan on serving about four wines, including a dry white wine, a medium-dry white wine and two red wines. The white wines should be well-chilled before serving, and you can use ice buckets to keep them pleasantly cool. For the red wines, allow them to come up to room temperature and open about a half hour before the guests are due, so that they can ''breathe,'' which allows their flavour to reach its peak.

Here are some good cheeses and the wines that complement them best:

Creamy cheese such as *Bel Paese, Pyrenees:*
French Loire wines, German wines, Italian *Soave*, California *Chenin Blanc*.
Swiss cheese, *Cantal, Gouda:*
Either a full white wine such as French *Burgundy*, or a light red such as *Beaujolais, Chianti*, or California *Gamay*.
Camembert, Brie, Munster:
Good with *Bordeaux* red wines, *Cotes du Rhone* or a really full white wine such as Australian *Semillon* or California *Chardonnay*.
Cheddar, Cheshire:
These salty cheeses need a fuller and smoother red wine such as French *Burgundy* or a heavier *Chateauneuf du Pape* or California *Zinfandel* or *Petite Sirah*.
Blue cheese such as *Roquefort;*
In France, these are sometimes served with a sweet dessert wine such as *Sauterne*, or try a smooth red wine with full flavour such as *Barbera* from Italy, or *Rioja* from Spain.

Offer plenty of crackers and bread with the cheeses, with creamy butter and perhaps a few raw vegetables such as celery sticks and carrot sticks as a complement.

A LUNCH PARTY

This may be elegant or casual, indoors or out. The main factor is to remember that this is the middle of the day and your drinks should be correspondingly light in alcohol. Avoid anything rich and creamy and go for long drinks with full flavour. If you are entertaining at home, try a **Mimosa**, made with sparkling wine, then follow up with wine or beer. Offer dry white wines and perhaps a rosé to accompany a light luncheon. A nice touch is to end a special lunch with a liqueur coffee, perhaps Irish Coffee, which is ideal in winter time. In summer, a long cool cocktail such as a **Bloody Mary** or **Harvey Wallbanger** is perfect to start. Follow this with **Cider Cup** or simply wine with orange juice and mineral water with the meal.

153

Black Russian

NORDIC PARTY

On a cold day, follow the example of the Scandinavians and warm yourself with some fiery spirits. Offer small glasses of well-chilled vodka or *aquavit* with good quality lager beer, and the option of one or two cocktails for those who like a slightly sweeter drink – perhaps a **Black Russian** and a **Moscow Mule**, to follow the theme! For food, try a selection of smoked fish such as herring and mackerel, with some stuffed vegetables. Make *Cucumber Appetizers* by scooping out the centre of a cucumber, after cutting it into manageable chunks. Leave a little flesh at the base to hold the filling, then cream together 6 ounces of cream cheese and 1 small carton of sour cream. Fill the cucumber sections with the mixture and top with diced pieces of smoked salmon. For *Stuffed Tomatoes* cut off the tops of the tomatoes and scoop out the centres. Mix chopped, cooked shrimp with mayonnaise (about 8 ounces of shrimp to 1½ cups mayonnaise), fill the tomatoes and replace the tops. For elegant *Salmon Cornets*, roll thinly-sliced smoked salmon around caviar into a cone shape.

Mimosa

CHAMPAGNE BREAKFAST
Here is a way of adding sparkle to an important weekend, or perhaps to Christmas or Thanksgiving celebrations. Have a late breakfast and serve sparkling wine with orange juice, **Bucks' Fizz** or **Mimosa** to your guests, as they sample various light foods such as smoked fish, scrambled eggs and grilled bacon.

CELEBRATIONS
For a party which celebrates some particular event, choose drinks to fit the occasion. For example, if it is New Year's Eve, offer some Scottish cocktails such as the **Rusty Nail** and **Rob Roy** for "Auld Lang Syne." For a graduation, a fruity punch would be ideal, while a wedding naturally calls for champagne. The **Champagne Cocktail** makes a marvellous toast if your guests are not too numerous. A christening means a getting together of all the family and offers a chance to serve some attractive non-alcoholic drinks like the **Tenderberry**. And why not celebrate George Washington's Birthday with a glass of Madiera?

155

TROPICAL PARTY

With so many lovely cocktails to choose from, why not plan a party around a tropical theme – Caribbean or Hawaiian? Serve the **Piña Colada**, the **Santiago**, the **Mai Tai** or **Planter's Punch**, and make the garnish really attractive. Use fresh pineapple shells when available in place of glasses and serve these rich drinks with straws and lots of fresh fruit decoration. For food, consider a barbecue with spare ribs or even a sucking pig. Beer is a good alternative beverage after one or two of these powerful cocktails (the **Zombie** is one of the most stunning), with fruit juices for the less adventurous. Raw vegetables served with a variety of dips make an ideal accompaniment to the first drink.

To make *Guacamole* (Avocado Dip), you will need two ripe avocadoes, ¼ cup of sour cream, a small grated onion and a half green pepper. Cut the green pepper into small strips and blanch in boiling water. Scoop out the avocado flesh and mash well with remaining ingredients to make a rough puree. Sprinkle with lemon juice and pepper and leave to chill before serving. Offer corn chips as an alternative to raw vegetables.

For *Shrimp Dip* you need a can of shrimps (5 oz.), ¼ cup milk, 1 cup mayonnaise, a couple of drops of Tabasco, a tablespoon Worcestershire sauce, one small onion (chopped), 8 oz. of cubed cheddar cheese and a little garlic salt. Combine these ingredients in the blender and blend well until smooth. Serve cool.

Piña Colada

HOW TO MAKE THE PARTY GO SMOOTHLY

Many people are reluctant to give a cocktail party because they doubt that they can mix drinks and keep an eye on guests as well. The secret is advance planning, and appointing someone as official bartender. For your first attempt at cocktails, invite a small number of guests, or plan a very informal get-together, perhaps outdoors.

Prepare all canapés and snacks well in advance, or arrange with someone to help with the assembly just before party time. Make sure that you have plenty of all the ingredients needed for the specific drinks you will serve .

If possible, mix up pitchers of certain drinks so that several people may be served at once, and then help themselves. **Martinis, Bloody Marys** and **Margaritas** may all be mixed like this. Any drink which is not mixed with ice cubes may be prepared in advance – ice dilutes the drink as it melts and spoils its flavour.

Glasses can be a problem. Although there is a wide range of ''appropriate'' glasses, it is easier to keep to a small selection – cocktail glasses, wine glasses and some tumblers, tall and short. These may be rented from your off-licence, providing you buy your party drinks there. Alternatively choose inexpensive glassware from your supermarket rather than using fine crystal. The point of a cocktail party is the style of the whole event, rather than individual fine details which are important for a dinner party. So make the drinks look pretty. You can even use plastic tumblers (very practical if you are entertaining outdoors).

You will need a good supply of ice so be sure you buy this in from a local supplier, if possible. If you have a fair-sized freezer, make ice in trays then transfer to plastic bags. Remember to start freezing at least two days before the party!

Credits
Editor: Jennifer Mulherin
Designer and Art Director: Tom Deas

Photographs by Simon Butcher
Stylist: Lyn Rutherford

Acknowledgements
Cocktail Shop, 30 Neal St,
Covent Garden, London WC2

Del Monico's, Wine and Spirit
Merchants, 64 Old Compton St,
London W1